THE DAY STAR AND US

DARRELL MOWAT

WESTBOW
PRESS®
A DIVISION OF THOMAS NELSON
& ZONDERVAN

WestBow Press books may be ordered through booksellers or by contacting:

WestBow Press
A Division of Thomas Nelson & Zondervan
1663 Liberty Drive
Bloomington, IN 47403
www.westbowpress.com
844-714-3454

Scripture taken from the King James Version of the Bible.

ISBN: 978-1-6642-4315-6 (sc)
ISBN: 978-1-6642-4314-9 (e)

Print information available on the last page.

WestBow Press rev. date: 08/18/2021

CONTENTS

PREFACE

When I was growing up, I was taught in school about the idea of "world" peace. How we should all get along. The United Nations, no doubt, had some influence in my school curriculum on the subject, and certainly Disney's, "It's a small world after all" song, made a huge impact not only on my life; but for the general view of this world in the 20th and early 21st centuries A.D., at least from my perspective. However, this subject is not a new one, and has been talked about for thousands of years. Many scholars and lay people alike have spoken of it. The phrase I have heard more than once as a child by my elders, "...slower than the 2nd coming", comes to mind. Is this not true? We have been told by Jesus, Old Testament prophets and the New Testament authors, that God is coming to establish His kingdom. The "Messianic Jews" are still waiting, and so are the Christians; other faiths are waiting for some sort of kingdom to come, and we are all trying to "figure out" what exactly is going to happen?

That is how this book came into being. I have learned, read, discussed, researched and started to develop an interpretation of what the Bible may be saying about the "...time of the end.", Christ's Kingdom and what God has instore for us into our future here on earth (Dan. 12:9). I should say, it is not really an interpretation, but rather a discussion of what God may have been suggesting, through the multitude of His prophets and God willing, His Holy Spirit's inspiration in the writing of this book. This book is a culmination of learning from various religious organizations' interpretations and teachings, "secular" world views, and making an effort to reconcile my own thoughts, with what the Bible says; kind of like "putting the pieces of the puzzle together". I should also say, that I do not and never will claim to have all of the answers regarding prophecy and what God has planned for the future of this world and mankind in general; but I like to think, that He does indeed have a plan and a good one at that!

In general, this book was written as if I did not necessarily need to be "around" for the "Messianic Age", as it is sometimes referred to as, to be fulfilled. Actually, it was written with the idea that God's Holy Spirit would be the main character or actor in bringing about God's Kingdom to earth. God forbid it be any other way. I wrote this book, keeping in mind, that it could serve as a kind of "handbook" of sorts, to direct the reader into what the "1000 year reign of Christ and His saints" may look like, and how it may be structured (Rev. 20:4, 6). That being said, I do not expect this book to be an end all guide on how the "world" should be "run", but to give some insight into what the Bible may be saying about what a time of peace here on earth may look like. With that in mind, open yourself up to considering the future and your part in it. How may it look for you, and your family, and their descendants, in the following centuries; until Christ "comes" or He calls us "home" (2 Cor. 5:16)?

If you have a relationship with God, or do not; if you believe or do not; this book is still for you. Even if you look at this book as purely fiction, you still may be able to glean some interesting information from it. This book has been written in such a way, that it should by the end of it, reach out to every person in this world, from every tribe, tongue and nation. Take time and read through the various chapters of this book, and ask yourself, where do I fit into this possible future or our present world for that matter? We have a wonderful Creator who has designed this world (Rom. 1:20). It may be a challenge to believe at times, but sometimes we just need to take that leap of faith and live (2 Cor. 1:24)! There is additional information that expands on certain topics in the chapters, at the end of the book, and, of course, the reader can always go to the Bible, which is the ultimate Book of truth in what God says about the past, present and future of this world, our lives and His creation forevermore. Read on to learn more!

ACKNOWLEDGEMENTS

A great amount of credit is due, to those whom have pioneered this topic of the "Messianic Age", both Jews and Christians alike. There are many individuals and organizations that believe in, celebrate and look forward to a time on earth of relative peace; but more than that, when the true God is worshipped by this entire world in spirit and in truth (John 4:23).

The Bible speaks about this time, also known as the "Millennial reign of Christ with His saints", in both the New and Old Testament's, and many people have written their comments on or interpretations of it (Rev. 20:4, 6). If this book's interpretation is at all, or mostly all correct; it is for the glory of God, the Father, and His only begotten Son, Jesus Christ of Nazareth, the Saviour of us all, with His Holy Spirit. The future is bright indeed. Praise the Lord!

INTRODUCTION

There has been much speculation amongst; Biblical scholars, theologians, students, disciples and even "laymen", of what Jesus and even the Old Testament prophets meant by the "Kingdom of God", the coming Kingdom, Heaven on earth, etc.. And I am sure there will still be unanswered questions on this for some time to come. The Jewish community have a concept of Tikkun Olam – "repairing the world"; that is very much supposed to be related to the idea of a literal "Messianic Age". Of such, the Bible does describe, and will be spoken about in this book, from a literal and "spiritual", Judeo-Christian perspective; with other cultures and religious viewpoints in mind. However, for the interested reader, there are three or four general "schools" of thought, from a Christian perspective, on the "Messianic Age", "Millennial reign of Christ with His saints", "God's kingdom on earth", etc.. They are Pre-, Post-, A- millennialism and Dispensationalism.

A-millennialism "does not teach a literal thousand-year earthly reign of Christ", but that it has been taking place "spiritually" since Christ's ascension approximately 2000 years ago. Pre-millennialism teaches "that Christ will come visibly to this earth before, or at the beginning of the millennium. At that time the saints will arise (first resurrection), and reign with Christ on earth one thousand years." (Rev. 20). And Post-millennialism says, "That there will be a millennium, but that Christ will return visibly, after the millennium. Where during the "millennium" the gospel will continue to be taught and the Church will grow.". These definitions are simplified compared to the expanded definitions of each of these terms, but the interested reader can look into the definitions further, for more insight. There is also a school called "dispensationalism" and it has something to do with a "reaction" to the Church of England by a fellowship named, the "Plymouth Brethren". They believe that earth's history is divided into 7 "dispensations" or periods of time, and that the 7th is the so called "Millennium". But again the interested reader can look into this "school" of thought at your leisure.

Nevertheless, this book does in some form, conform to each of these definitions, because there is likely some truth to all of them; but focuses more on a "what if the millennium was going to be literal?" and "how would it be experienced?" viewpoint. That being said, Peter spoke in 2 Peter 3:10, of the "…day of the Lord…come[ing] as a thief in the night; in the which the heavens shall pass away with great noise, and the elements shall melt with fervent heat, the earth also and the works that are therein shall be burned up.". A portion of this "…day of the Lord…" was mentioned in a book I have written, referencing the "Great Tribulation" spoken of in the Bible just before the "Millennial reign of Christ with His saints", it is called "Time, times and a dividing of time – What did John really see?" (Matt. 24, 2 Pet. 3:10). The references for that book, are spoken of in, the book of Revelation, Daniel and Ezekiel; all of which are in the canonized KJV of the Bible. So the question then stands, is the "Messianic Age" literal, or is God just going to finish His work on earth through some catastrophic event, without much notice to the unbelievers and believers alike? This is where faith comes in, because "…one day *is* with the Lord as a thousand years…", so this so called "…day of the Lord…", may be a day, a year and/or 1000 years (Ps. 90:4, Ezek. 4:6, 2 Pet. 3:8, 10). And after all is complete, however long that "…day…" is, God will indeed bring His final everlasting judgement, on this temporary earthly planet, and all those souls whom have ever inhabited it (Mal. 3:2, 2 Pet. 3:10, Rev. 20:11-15).

Last, as always, what is most important in understanding any Biblical concepts and possible prophetic words, is that we put it into proper perspective. We need to ask the question, how is this relevant to my relationship with God, my family and my community? Jesus Christ of Nazareth died for us on the cross for the forgiveness of our sins, shedding His Holy and righteous blood on the cross at Passover. He was buried and He arose the third day to give us a hope for our own bodily resurrection and eternal life in His Holy name (John 3:16). In this life, we need to focus on developing and growing our personal relationship with our Creator, and His creation, in order to fulfil our purpose here on earth. God loves us, and He gave His only begotten Son, Jesus Christ Immanuel of Nazareth, for us, so that whomsoever believes in Him will not perish, but will have everlasting life (John 3:16). With that in mind, let us pray to God, "Thy kingdom come." and trust in "…the peace of God, which passeth all understanding…", to guide us in this life until He "comes" or we are called "home" (Matt. 6:10, John 14:3, Phil. 4:7).

CHAPTER 1

THE PURPOSE

*"...I am come that they might have life, and that
they might have it more abundantly."*

– JOHN 10:10

Introduction

It has always been God's purpose that we live to be "...very good..." (Gen. 1:31). He created us that way (1 Cor. 6:19, 20). Of course, our ancestors fell, then the flood came to "baptize" their descendants, in a way (Gen. 3:1-7, 7:1-7). Then the Law came to guide us in a human way (Ex. 20:1-17, John 1:17, Rom. 5:20, Gal. 3:24). Then judges and kings came to reign over them (1 Sam. 8:1-5). Then finally, Christ came, to redeem us from the fall, in the beginning of humankind, here on earth (Matt. 5:17, Rom. 10:4, 1 Cor. 15:21, 22). Now we have a choice, choose Christ or follow our own "way" (Deut. 30:19). This has been the choice since the beginning, and we still have that choice today. God is calling us all, out of this world, out of its ways and back to Him (Jer. 51:45, 2 Cor. 6:17, Rev. 18:4).

The real purpose of this world, and life, in general, is to; establish or re-establish our relationship with our Creator, grow in the knowledge of Christ Jesus of Nazareth, and become children of God, so that we can indeed live forever (2 Cor. 3:18, Col. 3:9-11)! All of the trimmings, blessings, joys and trials that come along with this life, are great for the most part, but are temporary. We need to keep in mind the greater purpose of our lives, and that is to become children of God, in His Kingdom! As the Bible says, "...seek ye first the kingdom of God and his righteousness; and all these things shall be added unto you." (Matt. 6:33).

Good Relationships

Although this book talks about some things, such as a temple being built, and some "Old Testament" holydays being commonly observed. God is much greater and simpler than the commands of men (1 Cor. 1:25). In John 4, Jesus spoke to a Samaritan woman, whom was likely, at least partially descended, from those whom make up the northern 10 tribes of Israel (1 Kings 16:29, Isa. 7:9, Amos 3:12, Oba. 1:19). They got into a conversation, about where a person needs to worship, and Jesus said that there is a time that is coming and has come where we will need not go to this place or that place to worship, but that we will worship God in Spirit and in Truth (John 4:19-24). This is probably the most important point of this book, and it is; that God desires a personal relationship with each and every one of us through conversation, prayer; study, reading God's word; and praise and worship, thanksgiving; which can also be done through fellowship with others (Jos. 1:8, Ps. 69:30, 31; 145:18; Luke 18:1, Col. 4:2, 2 Tim. 3:16, 17)!

This is what Jesus and the commandments of the Old Testament taught. First is, to love God with all of our heart, mind and soul, and then to love our neighbour (Ex. 20:1-17, Luke 10:27). The 10 Commandments given at Mount Sinai, can be summed up in these two commands (Matt. 22:20). Starting or strengthening our relationship with God, through His Holy Spirit, is most important. God created us and He loves us; but He also desires us to love ourselves, not in an ungodly way, but through His Holy Spirit (Eph. 5:29). How can we love others, if we do not first, love ourself? Not to say that we should be selfish, greedy or manipulative; but that we should allow God to be kind to us (John 15:9, 2 Tim. 3:1, 2). The Bible says that God is good to all (Ps. 145:9). Then once we begin to realize that God loves us, and that He desires us to be loved and love, then we can reflect that love to others, in Christ we are perfected (Song 4:7, Heb. 10:14). This is the key; it all starts with God's relationship with us as individuals. God breathed life into a man, Adam, and he "…became a living soul.", then God took a rib from Adam and made the woman out of Adam, and Adam named her Eve (Gen. 1:27, 28; 2:7, 21-25; 3:20, 5:2). This is it, He desires an intimate relationship with each and every one of us, a living breathing relationship with us, He desires to be all in all (John 3:16, 1 Cor. 15:28, Eph. 4:6, Col. 1:17)!

Good Health

God's Holy Spirit is a clean, pure and healthy spirit (Ex. 15:26, Ps. 18:30, 51:10; Matt. 5:8, John 4:24). If or when the earth is encompassed by God's Holy Spirit, one can only imagine that those whom dwell in the earth will or are being healed. There are many verses that speak of God's healing in prophecy, nevertheless we can still experience this healing in our lives, as individuals, today (Isa. 53:5, 1 Pet. 2:24)! Jesus came to give us life and life more abundantly (John 10:10). God has been blessing, healing and providing for ALL people since the beginning of time (Ps. 145:9)! So literal "Messianic Age" reign of Christ or not, He can and will still give you good health, today (Jam. 5:16). The key is, following God's Holy Spirit (Prov. 3:1-9)!

There are an incredible number of healthy living ideas in this world; including types of food to eat, diet plans, exercise methods and frequency, etc.. But this is exactly what they are, worldly ideas; God does desire us to eat healthy, as there are health "laws" in the Bible; but we should not turn our own health or methods of health into a "god" or "idol" in and of itself, because then you may develop mental health problems that will end up bringing you down instead (Lev. 11). Jesus said, "…Take no thought for your life, what ye shall eat, or what ye shall drink; nor yet for your body, what ye shall put on. Is not the life more than meat, and the body than raiment?" (Matt. 6:25). In an epistle, it also says, that physical exercise profits little, but spiritual exercise profits much (1 Tim. 4:8). The important thing to remember is, that God desires us to think about ourselves, but also the people around us, and most importantly, about Him (Isa. 61:1-3, Ezek. 47:12)! If we constantly try to control our world around us; what we eat, what we wear, and how we maintain our strength; how are we going to learn how to trust in our Creator?

He will provide the necessary "plan" for eating right foods (Ex. 23:25). He will "plan" for daily or weekly exercise (Jer. 33:6). And He will plan for all your other needs, just let Jesus Christ of Nazareth in, to show you, what His desires are for you, in this area of life (Ex. 15:26). There are a couple verses, that should comfort a person, whom is trying to live a "healthier lifestyle", however. They are, "No weapon that is formed against thee shall prosper…" (Isa. 54:17). And also, the example of the apostle, Paul, whom was bitten by a poisonous snake and was not harmed (Acts 28:3-6). The point is, that the odds can be stacked against us as far as health goes, but God is still in the miracle business; this is where faith comes in. We need to follow God, first and foremost; a good example is of an Old Testament king whom trusted in "…physicians.", instead of the Lord; he died 2 years after his transgression, although he reigned 41 years in total (2 Chr. 16:12, 13). This is why God desires us to follow Jesus Christ of Nazareth, first and foremost, before any other "expert", including myself (Mal. 4:2)! God is the miracle Worker and Producer, not us (Lam. 3:37)!

And Love

The immoveable nature of God, is that He does not change (Num. 23:19, Ps. 33:11, Isa. 46:10). Malachi wrote of God, "For I *am* the LORD, I change not; therefore ye sons of Jacob are not consumed." (Mal. 3:6). He established seasons, days, years, ordinances, etc., and they do not change (Gen. 1:14, 8:22). God is good and always will be good (Ps. 100:5, 136:1). He is the solid Rock, in whom we can trust (2 Sam. 22:2, Ps. 62:6, Matt. 7:24). His love endures forever (1 Chr. 16:34). His love was revealed to man fully in Jesus Christ of Nazareth, God's only begotten Son. All that Jesus did was listen to His Father, and teach all of mankind, what true love is (John 5:19, 8:28, 12:49). He did not come in power and strength, initially, although He could have; He did not come in a roaring voice and anger, mostly, although He could have; He came in a humble, gentle child, born in the most simple of circumstances; He grew up, and died the most shameful death, on the cross for the forgiveness of our sins, shedding His Holy and righteous blood for us (Luke 2:7, Gal. 3:13, Phil. 2:6-8). And He did this all for those, whom were still in sin, us (Rom. 5:8)! And after His death, He was buried, and arose the third day for our hope and promise of eternal life in His Holy name. The God whom created mankind, slowly, but surely revealed Himself for whom He was and is; in Adam and Eve, then in the law and the prophets, and then in the only begotten Son of God, the Word, Jesus Christ of Nazareth, the Rock and cornerstone of the Church, and now in the Body of Christ, the Church of the living God with His Holy Spirit (Gen. 1:27, 5:1, 2; Matt. 21:11, Luke 16:16, 1 Cor. 10:4, 12:12, 27; Eph. 2:20, Heb. 1:1, 2; Phil. 2:5, 1 Tim. 3:15)!

I should mention, that some of this book speaks of what some may consider "Jewish" ideas or traditions. I will say that I have no "official" training in Judaism, and likely never will; but that is what makes the Bible and God's Holy Spirit so wonderful, anyone can obey and follow God, Jew or Gentile, alike (2 Cor. 1:21, 22, Eph. 1:13, Gal. 3:28, Col. 3:11). And in particular, the Bible says, both in the New and Old Testament, that you are a Jew, if you are circumcised in the heart, meaning that God's Holy Spirit lives in you, and guides you (Deut. 30:6, Jer. 4:4, Rom. 2:29). People can put on outward appearances of "godliness", including myself; but God cares most about what is inside, what we desire, think about, long for, etc. (1 Sam. 16:7, Jer. 17:10). We need to understand that God is love (1 John 4:8). Jesus said, "Greater love hath no man than this, that a man lay down his life for his friends." (John 15:13). This is what Jesus did for us (1 John 3:16). The apostle, John, wrote, "There is no fear in love; but perfect love casteth out fear…", and that "Herein is love, not that we loved God, but that he loved us, and sent his Son *to be* the propitiation for our sins.", in Jesus Christ of Nazareth (1 John 4:10, 18). There are many more scriptures that describe love; but Jesus said, if we are to love Him, we are to follow His commands, His way, His example; That is love (John 14:15-23, 1 Cor. 13:4-8, 1 John 4:10-16).

I had been told when I first started earnestly seeking God and His desires for me, that I should read the gospel according to John. I think this was wise advice. John had a certain gift of the Holy Spirit, that I do not believe the other apostles had necessarily. His writings and communication are very "spiritual", and I think this was done on purpose (John 3:6, 6:63; 1 John 2:27). He is one of the pillars of the New Testament church, but he was also gifted with the vision of prophecy of things to come; seemingly more so than the others, as he physically authored the Book of Revelation (Rev. 1:1-7). For the beginner of Bible reading, I would definitely suggest reading the Gospel according to John; it is like reading poetry, in a sense. As John wrote, "In the beginning was the Word and the Word was with God and the Word was God. The same was in the beginning with God. All things were made by him; and without him was not any thing made that was made." (John 1:1-3).

Conclusion

The remainder of this study is going to talk about some of the changes that may take place, and what certain infrastructure, worship methods and governing changes may take place here on earth when or if a literal "Messianic Age" or 1000 year reign of Christ with His saints, comes

(Rev. 20:4, 6). There ought not to be any mystery or secrets here (Amos 3:7, Matt. 10:26). The key is, to follow God's Holy Spirit. God, no doubt, is practical (Eccl. 11:3). He does not and will not change (Mal. 3:6). His plan has always been the same, since the beginning, and will, no doubt, remain the same throughout eternity (Num. 23:19). With that being said, keep in mind and open yourself up to the ideas and plan God may have for you, in this life; as we are all peculiarly created by our Maker for His purpose, glory and for our own enjoyment in Christ, as well (Ex. 19:5, Rom. 8:28, Eph. 3:11, 2 Tim. 1:9, 1 John 3:8). We are not slaves, but fellow heirs; follow Jesus Christ of Nazareth and He will give you the desires of your heart (Ps. 37:4, 5; Prov. 16:9, Matt. 6:21, 33; Rom. 8:17).

Discussion: Rest

"So when the Man comes there will be no, no doom."
- Bob Marley, One Love

It is interesting the world we live, as of the early 21st century A.D.; so many people, from so many different cultures, religions, languages and nations. How can we possibly all get along? When I was younger, I used to listen to Bob Marley quite a bit, namely during my secondary school days. Although I do not necessarily agree with all of his methods and "philosophies", he was certainly something of a prophet. I am sure he must have read the Bible, and, of course, that comes out in his lyrics to some of his music. Although we must be careful whom we listen to outside of the Bible, and the Holy Spirit; the Bible does admonish to "…believeth all things…" (1 Cor. 13:7). That being said, even as Christ followers, we should not toss aside the "secular" world completely; we are to come out of the world, but God can still work through it, and needs us to live in it; this is where discernment of spirits comes in (John 17:18, 1 Cor. 12:10)!

Discussion Questions

1. Some time ago an idea came into my head; that worship was going to be the method in which evil would be cast from earth. Now there are many forms of worship, and you may desire to learn what forms best suit you; but something is to be said about enjoying pleasant music. David calming king Saul's spirit with a harp, is a perfect example (1 Sam. 16:23). With that being said; how can you contribute in a simple way to the praise and worship of your Creator?

_____

_____

_____

2. In this physical world, some of the best ways we consider to be healthier is by eating properly, exercising and working safely. These are all very important acts, we can partake in, to take care of our body; but ultimately we need to nourish our spirit and soul, first and foremost (Matt. 6:25, Matt. 10:28, Rom. 14:17). What type of habits can be started, renewed or grown, that nourish your soul, mind and body? (Hint: Thanksgiving and Prayer are a great start).

_____

_____

_____

3. What are some forms of love, that we can portray to this world, to show God's love? Review 1 Corinthians 13 to get started.

_____

_____

_____

CHAPTER 2

THE PEOPLE

"…greater is he that is in you, than he that is in the world."

– 1 JOHN 4:4

Introduction

This chapter is purposed, to reach out to a generation or generations of people, that may indeed see the fruits of the ideas of this book, come to pass. It is challenging to say for sure, what the future has in store for us, but we can get glimpses of possibilities of the future through obedience to God and allowing Him to reveal knowledge to us through His Word and in TRUE Signs and Wonders (Isa. 8:18, Dan. 2:28, Amos 3:7, 2 Cor. 12:12, Matt. 10:26). This requires faith, but you need not worry about that either, because God gives us the faith that we need, as well (Eph. 2:8)! So with that being said; I will speak about who these people whom may experience the "Messianic Age", might be, where they may come from, what makes them different; and what they may have to "…endure…" to experience the "Messianic Age" on earth (Matt. 10:22)!

Who are they?

I should first say, that I have no doubt, that we can, indeed, experience God's Kingdom here on earth, whether there is a literal "Messianic Age" or not. God gives to us, His peace and abundance, through our obedience to Him (Prov. 3:1, 2; 1 Pet. 1:2, 2 Pet. 1:2). This is the key, "Who are God's people?". They are the people who listen to, seek out, and obey God's Counsel! So the question, "who are they?", is a rather mysterious one; because anyone can be listening to God, as it says in the New Testament (Rom. 2:14, 15). The Bible also says, that "…if thou shalt confess with thy mouth the Lord Jesus, and shalt believe in thine heart that God hath raised him from the dead, thou shalt be saved." (Rom. 10:9, 1 John 4:15). The apostle, John, said it even more simply, in that "Whosoever shall confess that Jesus is the Son of God, God dwelleth in him, and he in God." (1 John 4:15). Do you believe?

Nevertheless, there must be some clear sign of those whom are obedient to Christ, compared to those whom are not; or else how would we "know" whom to listen to, unless we had an extremely close relationship with God, through His Holy Spirit, dwelling in us? This is another key! Reading God's Word and listening to others is great; but if we do not trust God, and allow His Holy Spirit, to dwell in our body, mind and soul; we are going to have a challenging time obeying Him and experiencing an enduring, lasting peace. Ezekiel 11:13-21 talks about God's remnant in a very candid manner; and in particular, it points to the truth of God's prophecies being fulfilled. Namely, verse 17 says, that a remnant would return to the ancient lands that Israel once dwelt in, which HAS been taking place, over the last 100 years or so, as of the early 21st century A.D.! Indeed God's Word is truth, and His commands are and will be fulfilled! Ezekiel 14:22 and Micah 4:5-8 also describe some of the characteristics of these people. Micah 4 speaks of the "…halted…" becoming a remnant, and those whom were "…cast far off…" becoming a strong nation!

Last, 1 Corinthians 2:9 says, "…Eye hath not seen, nor ear heard, neither have entered into the heart of man, the things which God hath prepared for them that love him.". A great promise, for anyone whom is looking to God for answers! And we always have the faithful promise of Christ returning to us, in and through us, to save us with His Holy Spirit (1 Cor. 6:19)! Hebrews 9:28 says, "…and unto them that look for him shall he appear the second time without sin unto salvation."! This is the last key, put your faith in Jesus Christ Immanuel of Nazareth for your salvation, He is the only begotten Son of God (Isa. 7:14, 9:6; Matt. 1:23, Acts 4:12, Rom. 1:16, 1 John 4:15). He died on the cross for the forgiveness of our sins, shedding His Holy and righteous blood. He was buried, and He arose from the dead on the third day, for your justification (Rom. 3:24, 1 Cor. 15:4)!

Where do they come from?

Remnant in the Bible, may mean "descendants", also; Strong's number 7611. This can be seen in Ezekiel 9:8, when Ezekiel is speaking with God and asking Him if He intends to destroy the entire remnant or "…residue…" of Israel. Of course, this was regarding an event that was taking place in Ezekiel's time; but the term, remnant of Israel, is still relevant today! If you believe what the Bible says, then we all came from somewhere; namely, from Adam and Eve. Now, if you know anything about the flood account; Noah came out from the ark, with his three sons; Japheth, Shem and Ham, with their wives and Noah's wife. All three of his sons had descendants born to them, after the flood (Gen. 9:18, 19). Now, Shem was "special", in that his lineage was to continue the righteous blood of Abel, Seth, Enoch, Noah, etc. (Gen. 4:25, 9:26; Luke 3:23-38, Heb. 11:4-7). This continued with Abraham, Isaac, and finally, Jacob; whom became named Israel by God, and he had twelve sons; one of whom had two sons, also blessed by Jacob, and later, all blessed by Moses after their sojourn in Egypt (Gen. 35:1048, 49; Deut. 33). These 12 sons and their descendants, unto today; are whom God is referring to when He says, "…remnant of Israel…" (Ezek. 11:13). He is referring to the descendants of the 12 sons of Israel; the "Tribes" of Israel, whom still inhabit the earth today! And have become a great people and nations of peoples, indeed; as prophesied and blessed by God through Jacob and later blessed by Moses, during their sojourn in the wilderness after leaving Egypt!

That all being said, God is still calling people from every nation, tribe and tongue, to become a part of His "heavenly" or "eternal" family (Rev. 7:9). This was the purpose of the finished work of Jesus Christ of Nazareth, whom was and is a descendant of one of the 12 tribes of Israel; namely Judah, through His earthly mother, Mary, but was also before all nations, because of His heavenly Father's eternal existence (Luke 3:23-38, John 8:58)! Jesus was and is the Son of God! He had no earthly father in the sense that he was not conceived by an earthly man; He was conceived, by God, the Holy Spirit in the virgin Mary, espoused to Joseph (Matt. 1:18, Luke 1:35)! The point is, that although God does indeed have a "chosen people", namely the descendants of the tribes of Israel. He is still calling and working through people of all nations, tribes and tongues, here on earth today. God sent His only begotten Son, Jesus Christ of Nazareth, to save ALL of mankind (John 3:16). However, the promises of the blessings, do still remain today, for the descendants of the tribes of Israel, and will continue forever, if we obey Him in them (1 Chr. 17:27). So if you think your ancestors are of Hebrew or Israelite origin; take heart and believe that your God is with you (Jos. 1:9)! I will speak more about the subject of the descendants of Israel, in another book, but there are at least a few published books available on the subject; searching the internet for "history of the tribes of Israel book" will likely bring promising results.

Nevertheless, Jeremiah and Ezekiel speak candidly about where the remnant of Israel comes from, and what God's plan is for them. The interested person may be wise to read them (Jer. 23:3-8, Ezek. 36, 37). Jeremiah 23:5 in particular, talks about "…a King…" reigning over them. This is, no doubt, referencing Jesus Christ of Nazareth; but I will get into the "literal" interpretation of "…a King…" reigning over them in chapter four, and you can also see appendix B for details of the "…Branch…" referenced in Jeremiah 23:5 (Ezek. 16:60, 34:23-31; Acts 13:32-41, 1 Cor. 1:30). In the New Testament, James address's the tribes of Israel, he says, "James, a servant of God and of the Lord Jesus Christ, **to the twelve tribes** which are **scattered abroad**, greeting." (Jam. 1:1). Jesus asked His disciples to reach out to the "…lost sheep of the house of Israel…" specifically; and He gave them, the apostles, judgment over the 12 tribes of Israel, in His kingdom (Matt. 10:6, 15:24; Luke 22:30). Referencing Luke 22:30, the apostles will likely be in spirit form during the "Messianic Age", if literal; judging "behind the scenes" or this might be referring to the final judgment at the end of this earth's present history, in general (Matt. 19:28, Titus 3:5, Rev. 20:11-13). However, we can well imagine and believe that what God says, will happen, as He wills it (John 6:38-40). Just like on earth, responsibilities do not rest solely on one person's shoulders; God also can and does delegate responsibilities in His eternal kingdom. Jesus has a big job to do, and He needs us all to help Him with it!

What makes them different?

The difference mainly is that the remnant will follow the Judeo-Christian God of the Bible, the God of Israel, the God of Isaac, Abraham and Shem (Gen. 9:26, Ex. 3:6, Luke 1:68). That being said, the Bible does speak about "…a remnant according to the election of grace." (Rom. 11:5). This remnant is generally located in the north western hemisphere of the earth, as of the early 21st century A.D.; but is also scattered abroad, through the colonisations, that have taken place, over the last few thousand years, from the various empires, that have successfully circumnavigated the globe. They are the men and women, and their descendants, whom have followed the God of the Bible; through worship, strife, patience, wars, and trials of all kinds, throughout history, but have always been delivered by God Almighty, through His gently, mercifully guiding hand (Ps. 132). They are the men and women, that Jesus Christ of Nazareth came to save, the "…lost sheep…" of Israel, "…scattered abroad…"; this started when the Northern Tribes of Israel divided with Judah, because of King Solomon of Judah and the Northern tribes idolatries, alike (1 Kings 11, 12; Matt. 10:6, Jam. 1:1). But they were prophesied to come together again, first spiritually, through Jesus Christ of Nazareth, and then likely literally, in the "Messianic Age" (Ezek. 37, Matt. 10:6, 15:24; John 3:16).

Although, not a prerequisite, because of the pre-eminence in salvation through faith in Jesus Christ of Nazareth, the Redeemer (Eph. 2:8). This "…remnant…" and "…great multitude…", may have at least considered, if not turned completely from heathen festivals and ways of the world, to God's Holy days, rules and laws (Ex. 20:1-17, Lev. 23, Deut. 4:29, Isa. 10:17-22, Jer. 23:20, 30:24; Ezek. 45:13-25, Matt. 5:18, Rev. 7:9-14, 11:13)! Colossians 2:16 and 17 says, "Let no man therefore judge you in meat, or in drink, or in respect of an holyday, or of the new moon, or of the Sabbath *days:* Which are a shadow of things to come; but the body *is* of Christ."! Deuteronomy 11:18-21 commands us to read, and remember God's Word, the Holy Bible; in our mind, and in our hand, literally reading it, and teaching the Bible to our children, all the day. And wherever we go, whatever we are doing, we are to speak godly words and wisdom, that is to speak through the Holy Spirit, not impure and foul words and curses. This is also admonished in the New Testament (Matt. 12:36, 37; Luke 6:28, 2 Tim. 2:16, Eph. 4:15). In general, obedience to God gives us, and our children, a long life, as "…heaven upon the earth." (Deut. 11:21, Heb. 13:20, 21)! Therefore, the remnant will have likely repented and turned from their sin, in obedience to God and His way of living, which is of blessings, abundance and peace (John 10:10). How could a person not desire this?

Last, 1 Peter 2:9 says, "But ye *are* a CHOSEN generation, a ROYAL priesthood, an HOLY nation, a peculiar people; that ye should shew forth the praises of him who hath called you out of darkness into his marvellous light…" – A KINGDOM of PRIESTS! Exodus 19:6 says the same, "And ye shall be unto me a kingdom of priests, and an holy nation. These *are* the words which thou shalt speak unto the CHILDREN of ISRAEL." – God is speaking to you! David's physical descendants, likely continue to maintain the throne status of Israel on the earth, as stated in the Bible, even if we do not recognize them (Ps. 24:1, 89:4; Luke 1:32). As, David loved God's commands and laws (Ps. 119:97)! And, if literal, and in the future, in the "Messianic

Age", this reign could be done by David's physical descendants', or descendants' from one of the other tribes of Israel. However, we must first remember, that Jesus Christ of Nazareth, has established David's throne, FOREVER, through His own life, His death on the cross for the forgiveness of our sins, His burial, and His resurrection three days later; assuring that no one can remove God's sovereign authority over earth or heaven, FOREVER (2 Sam. 12:13, 16; Isa. 9:6,7; Matt. 1:1, Luke 1:31-33)! The subject of a future "physical ruler" will be spoken of in chapters four and five; and you can see appendix B for more detail. Nevertheless, Jesus did not just come for David, or David's descendants, or even the tribes of Israel and their descendants only, for that matter. He came for EVERYONE, the entire world (John 3:16)!

If you are asking, what do I do now? The answer is in 1 Peter 2:9, you "…should shew forth the praises…" of God! Praise Him! Worship Him! Listen to Him! And obey Him and Him alone! How simple it is to follow the true and righteous God and King of Israel! Blessed be His Holy name! Jesus put it simply, all the law and the prophets are summed up in this, "Thou shalt love the Lord thy God with all thy heart, and with all thy soul, and with all thy mind. This is the first and great commandment. And the second is like unto it, Thou shalt love thy neighbour as thyself. On these two commandments hang all the law and the prophets." (Matt. 20:37-40). He put it even more simply in stating that, "So in everything, do to others what you would have them do to you, for this sums up the Law and the Prophets." (Matt. 7:12). And the apostle, John, said, "Herein is love, not that we loved God, but that he loved us, and sent his Son *to be* the propitiation for our sins." (1 John 4:10). This is the key, God loves us! He gave His only begotten Son, Jesus Christ of Nazareth, for us and He desires us to accept Jesus Christ of Nazareth, and follow Him, with His Holy Spirit (Matt. 4:19, 9:9, 19:21; 1 Pet. 2:21)!

What must they endure?

Jesus said, "But he that shall endure unto the end, the same shall be saved." (Matt. 24:13). This is the simplest explanation of what is required of us, to live for Christ; that is, to persevere in trials and place our trust in Jesus Christ of Nazareth, to the end (Heb. 12:2). Zephaniah 3:8-13, gives a great synopsis of what a person may have to "…endure…" to come into the "Messianic Age"; in verse 8 God says, "…WAIT ye upon me…" (Zeph. 3:8, Matt. 24:13)! And Zechariah 8:16 and 17 talk about what God is looking for in us; that is, to speak the truth and "…execute the judgment of truth and peace…" in our gates or courts! This world is not currently under the pure influence of God, as of the early 21st century A.D.. There are men and women whom are deceived and follow after their own wicked desires (Gen. 8:21, Matt. 15:19). The Bible says, when the coming of the Son of Man is, it will be like the days of Noah, everything will seem normal, but things will happen suddenly (Matt. 24:37-39). Not to mention, God said that the "…wickedness of man *was* great…" in the earth by the time the flood took place (Gen. 6:5).

Aside from this, I have written a book, that attempts to detail a time that will likely come just before the "Messianic Age", if indeed it is literally in the future, as of the early 21st century A.D..

It is called, "Time, Times and dividing of Time – What did John really see?". That book may be useful, if you are interested in understanding the subject of God's prophesied judgment on this earth, in greater detail, and how the earth may "…change…" before the prophesied "Messianic Age" (1 Cor. 15:51). That being said, there is sufficient information in the Holy Bible about God's "…wrath…", the "Great Tribulation" and tribulation, in general, for the interested reader (Zeph. 1:15, 16; Matt. 24:21, 29; John 3:36, Rom. 1:18, Rev. 7:14). The Good News is, for those whom believe; Jesus' blood has protected us from God's wrath (Rom. 5:9, 1 Thess. 5:9). This world as it stands, in the early 21st century A.D., is not 100% seeking God's will; in general, the human mind without God, is nothing more than that of an animal (Rom. 8:7, Col. 1:21, 2 Pet. 2:12, Jude 1:10). This is why we need God; we need Him to keep us sound, sane and alive. But the joy of following God is peace, abundance and life everlasting!

We must continue to put our trust in God, and His plan for us; in order to please Him, and ultimately receive and experience that peace, that most of us long for in our life, with God and others (Prov. 3:5-6). This can be done through a daily relationship with God; through prayer, and reading His Word, and fellowship with other believers, family, etc.; whom help strengthen our relationship with our Creator, and each other (Prov. 27:17)! However, the most important, thing is to know that God's Holy Spirit dwells IN you! All this requires, is an invitation, and acceptance through prayer, and testimony! The Bible says, that whomsoever confesses that Jesus is Lord and believes that God raised Him from the dead, they will be saved (Rom. 10:9, 1 John 4:15). John said it even more simply, in that "Whosoever shall confess that Jesus is the Son of God, God dwelleth in him, and he in God." (1 John 4:15). Do you believe? Also, water baptism is an outward display of accepting the Holy Spirit into our life, as well (Matt. 3:11, 16, 28:19; Mark 16:16, John 3:5, Acts 2:38, 10:47; 1 Cor. 6:11, 1 Pet. 3:21, Gal. 3:27). But as I have often heard, keep it simple stupid, KISS. If you are unsure of your salvation, just talk to someone you trust about it, things will work out! God loves you!

Conclusion

Revelation 19:15 says, "…he shall rule…with a rod of iron…" (Rev. 19:15). This is speaking of Jesus Christ of Nazareth, ruling the nations of the world. The key to understanding this verse is; what did he mean by "…rod of iron…" (Rev. 19:15)? Well there are some clues in the Old Testament; Jeremiah 10:16, calls Israel "…the rod…". It is mentioned again in Jeremiah 51 and goes into greater detail of how Israel is the "…the rod…" (Jer. 51:19-23). Namely, Israel, the 12 tribes and their descendants, are His warriors and disciplinarians; this can be seen throughout history, but especially noted, is when Israel had to openly take the land of Canaan from the former inhabitants, and remove them in order to cleanse it of its idolatry (Deut. 7:1-6, Jos. 6, etc.). Nevertheless, there is more to this, in a spiritual sense; because God's Word is so powerful, He can produce miracles, without even using human hands to scatter or destroy the enemy (Ps. 33:6, Ex. 23:7, Isa. 11:4, Heb. 11:3). The point is, that a portion of that "…rod…" may also be considered God's Word, His Holy Spirit, whom works in and through us, and anyone whom will allow Him into their life (Isa. 10:17, 11:1; Rev. 19:13, 15, 21)! That being said, Jesus is alive and well. God's Holy Spirit will work the way He wills it, not by our own will. So we will need to watch and pray, to understand the reality of any of these truths today or in things to come!

Again, in Revelation 5:9 and 10, it says of Jesus, "…thou wast slain, and hast redeemed us to God by thy blood out of every kindred, and tongue, and people, and nation; And hast made us unto our God kings and priests: and we shall reign on the earth.". Is this not proof, that God will be working through all of mankind, if indeed there is a literal, 1000 year reign of Christ with His saints? More will be talked about regarding Christ and the saints "roles", in the "Messianic Age" in chapter four. Nevertheless, if this verse is translated correctly, the proof must be there, that God is calling and choosing people from every, tongue, tribe and nation. This would fit perfectly with God's desire for ALL of mankind to be saved (John 3:16, 1 Tim. 2:4, 2 Pet. 3:9). To understand God's relationship with any of us, the interested person would be keen to read 2 Peter 1:16-21. The apostle, Peter, says, "…TAKE HEED, as unto a light that shineth in a dark place, UNTIL the day dawn, and the DAY STAR ARISE IN YOUR HEARTS…" (2 Pet. 1:19). Do you want that Day Star, Jesus Christ of Nazareth, to arise in your heart? If He has not already, He will; just invite Him in. As Jesus said, "Behold, I stand at the door, and knock: if any man hear my voice, and open the door, I will come in to him, and will sup with him, and he with me." (Rev. 3:20).

Last, I have read of peoples' testimonial experiences of their visits to Israel. It seems, that they have described in many cases, a "Messianic Age" type atmosphere, of peace and, more importantly, God's presence; in spite of what the news may indicate at times, in the early 21st century A.D.. If this is to be a taste of what the entire world will be experiencing, if indeed the "Messianic Age", is literal; then we certainly have a great standard to look forward to. That being said, we can experience this peace or "Messianic Age" type atmosphere, wherever we are here on earth today, and forever more, through a relationship with Christ Jesus of Nazareth and His Holy Spirit dwelling with us, amongst us and in us (Ezek. 11:16, Matt. 28:20, John 14:16)! This is the gift of God, as the Bible says, "…flesh and blood cannot inherit the kingdom of God…" (Eph. 2:8, 1 Cor. 15:50). We or our descendants, may very well come to see and experience a time of relative peace and prosperity worldwide; but the Kingdom of God is, first and foremost, spiritual; it starts in our heart; mind, body and soul (1 Cor. 2:16, Phil. 2:5)!

Discussion: No Other Name!

"Be the change you want to see in the world."
– Mahatma Ghandi

I have mentioned Mahatma Ghandi in my other writing, and he is indeed a very interesting character. He was a part of a movement that, generally, used non-violence, as a method of influence to remove a colonizing "power" from his country of birth. Not everything was always "perfect"; he fasted at times, because of violence, and he did eventually die from some opposition. But, he was an example of a servant for a cause, as Jesus Christ of Nazareth was, and is, a servant of God and for man, whom very much suggested to His own disciples, to change; a better word being "repent"; that involves mercy, forgiveness, mourning and turning from our sins to God, the Father, and Jesus Christ of Nazareth, the only begotten Son of God, with His Holy Spirit (Matt. 3:8, 4:17, 20:28, John 15:5)! I think Mahatma Ghandi was basically saying do not be a hypocrite. We can talk all we desire about change, and what should happen, but if we do not change ourselves, then we are just as Jesus would say, "…hypocrites…" (Matt. 23:13). Following God, listening to and obeying His Holy Spirit, is a lifelong conversion process; Ghandi was not perfect and had to learn from his errors, but Jesus was, and is, that perfect servant, leader. That is why we need and have Jesus Christ of Nazareth. He was, and is, that perfect example of a Man to follow; but He was more than a man, He was, and is, the only begotten Son of God. We have Him to follow unto our final day here on earth, and then God willing, unto eternal life in Jesus Christ of Nazareth, at our resurrections, like He has had His (Rom. 8:28-31, Col. 1:15, 16)! This is the one promise and gift not given by any other person here on earth; only in Jesus Christ of Nazareth, do we have eternal life, in His life giving sacrifice on the cross (John 11:25)! We need Jesus Christ of Nazareth to change our mind, body and soul, to receive the glory He received; so that we can also become like Him, children of God, as God created us to be from the beginning (Luke 3:28, 20:36, Rom. 6:23)! As the Bible says, "Neither is there salvation in any other: for there is none other name under heaven given among men, whereby we must be saved." (Acts 4:12). Jesus Christ of Nazareth is that Name above all names, at which every knee should bow and every tongue should confess that Jesus is Lord (Phil. 2:9-11)!

Discussion Questions

1. When referring to the "…remnant of Israel…", who might the Bible be talking about regarding these people (Ezek. 11:13)? Read Zephaniah 3 to start.

_____

_____

_____

2. If we as God's people are "called" to keep His appointed feast days, mentioned in Leviticus 23. How can we do so, if we are part of a congregation or ecclesiastical organization that does not necessarily outwardly or openly keep these commands on the church calendar?

_____

_____

_____

3. God says, in the Bible, in various places what will take place in the "...time of the end." (Dan. 12:9). Namely, that He will speak to us in dreams and visions. Although this has been confirmed to have been taking place since the beginning of Christ's resurrection, and even in the Old Testament, through the prophets and kings, etc.; it no doubt continues to take place today. How is God speaking to you? Do you have dreams or "visons" or ideas when resting that may be providing understanding for your future and the future of your loved ones? How should you act on them? Read Acts 2:17 and Joel 2:28 for more insight!

_____

_____

_____

CHAPTER 3

REBUILD, RESTRUCTURE AND REDISTRIBUTE

*"And hath made of one blood all nations of men for to dwell
on all the face of the earth, and hath determined the times
before appointed, and the bounds of their habitation…"*

– ACTS 17:26

Introduction

Although I have a civil engineering degree, and some knowledge of the world and its plights as it stands, in the early 21st century A.D.. I do not claim to be an expert on what the world must be like 100, 500 or 1000 years from now. But I can say this much; that we have the technology, manpower and resources to distribute affluence to the four corners of the earth, if we all got along and worked together. Easier said than done, of course; but the point is, that the current world financial and political structure does not seem to allow for this to be the case. Is any one person to be blamed? I think not, but we all must take on the burden of equality together (Ezek. 18:25, 29, 33:17, 20). As God said in the beginning, He created everything to be "…very good…" and mankind was made in His image, after His likeness (Gen. 1:27, 31). How can equality be brought about? Well, as it says in Ezekiel 33:20; judgement is the plan, truth, justice and righteousness; these actions will bring forth equality in the end (Rev. 20:11-5). God is the truth, and He desires justice for the poor, the widow and the fatherless, and for righteousness to prevail (Jam. 1:27)! In Jesus Christ of Nazareth with God, the Father, and God's Holy Spirit; equality is and will continue to be the goal amongst all social, economic, language, culture and ethnic "barriers", forever more!

We struggle with so much in this world in the early 21st century A.D., alongside mission trips, food distribution and educational structures being built; we unfortunately see, slavery of every kind, abuse, murder, tyranny, corruption and the like. This was the nature that entered man after our ancestors chose to turn away from God, in the garden of Eden (Gen. 2:17, 3:1-7). This nature first manifested itself, in the jealous and murderous act of Cain, against his brother Abel (Gen. 4:1-16). What is the point? If we were all to realize where we came from and turn from the fallen behaviour, we might all be able to better get along. Think, "It's a small world after all". Of course, this is not just going to come about by itself, but God will bring it about in His good time if and when He wills it. You can read more about events, that may lead up to the time of the "Messianic Age" in my book, "Time, Times and a Dividing of Time – What did John really see?", if you are interested. That all being said, God's Word speaks in more than one place, of the fact that the "…poor…" will always exist (Deut. 15:11, Matt. 26:11, etc.). And going further, God says, that the "…meek…shall inherit the earth." (Matt. 5:5). The point is, that physical wealth is not necessarily the goal, even in a time of peace on earth; having a right relationship with God and others is, however (Isa. 55:6)!

Rebuilding

After the catastrophic events of the "Great Tribulation", mentioned in my earlier publication, "Time, Times and a Dividing of Time – What did John really see?", also referenced throughout the Bible, especially in the Book of Revelation. Is it any wonder that this world, most likely the majority of it, will require rebuilding of some kind or another? This alone, could be a 1000 year project, but some evidence from previous world wars would show that humanity is fairly resilient when it comes to cleaning up and rebuilding after catastrophes. Thank God! Ezekiel 39 is a very good starting point, for what will be required at the onset of the "Messianic Age"; that is the burying of the dead, the destruction of weapons by using them as fuel, and the redistribution of wealth or inheritance, "…spoil…", from those whom have passed (Ezek. 39:9-11). These ideas are expanded upon, in chapter six of the book, "Time, Times and a Dividing of Time – What did John really see?". As the chapter title is called, simply put, it is "Clean-up time".

Another project may be, the Temple building spoken of in the later chapters of Ezekiel; that seems to be a prophecy yet to be fully fulfilled, as well, as of the early 21st century A.D. (Ezek. 40-46). There is some suggestion that king Herod started to restore the temple, that Zerubbabel rebuilt, based on some of the descriptions in Ezekiel's vision. But any side by side comparison of the "actual" scale models of the temple mentioned in Ezekiel, and king Herod's restored temple, do not come very close in comparison. Some indicators for timelines of the building of a temple can be found in Ezra, when Zerubbabel was instructed to rebuild in the time of the Babylonian exile (Ezra 3:1, 6, 8, 6:16). It took them a while to rebuild because of the enemies' disruptions, and other distractions; but once they started building they did eventually finish. And they even started offerings before the completion of the temple (Ezra 3:6). Nevertheless, our order of service to God should be; worship and praise, study and instruction and then action (Ps. 69:30, 31; Prov. 19:20, Jam. 1:19). If a temple is to be built, similar to this in the future, much consideration needs to be taken before it begins. You can read more about the Temple written about by Ezekiel, in chapter five, and you can see appendices B and G for more details.

The "…city…, The LORD is there.", is another more important aspect of the "Messianic Age" (Ezek. 48:35). Although not very big, by comparison to most cities today, approximately 1.65 x 1.65 miles squared (Ezek. 48:15-17). It is said to be the place of the Lord's throne, as well; the temple being the "other" location (Jer. 3:17, Joel 3:21, Zech. 2:10, 8:3; Rev. 21:3). In particular, Ezekiel speaks of the city being served by members of each of the tribes of Israel (Ezek. 48:19). If I had to guess, this is probably because it is representative of the whole house of Israel in the "Messianic Age". It is interesting where it is located, with respect to the remainder of the land division; being at the border of Judah and Benjamin's land allotments; see appendix D. It is mentioned that the city has gates, named for the twelve tribes of Israel, all around (Ezek. 48:31-34). I would suspect that the gates, at least in the South and North, may be used for visitors to enter and exit, when they are traveling to Jerusalem to visit the Temple during the Feast of Tabernacles in the "Messianic Age" (Zech. 14:16). I would suspect, as well, that this city would be the "capital" city of Israel, during this time, if not the entire world; as that is where the Lord is (Ezek. 48:35)! Regardless, there is undoubtedly, a very important plan and place for this city, in the time known as the "Messianic Age".

In referencing the dimensions of the land distribution and the location of the temple in the "Messianic Age" with respect to the "…city…"; see appendix E (Ezek. 48:35). The distance between the temple and city may be up to, approximately 4 to 5 miles, away from each other. This fact is very interesting, because if you look at a map, and start at the current location of the temple mount today, you come close to or around Bethlehem! Now, this is very important, because like everything else that the Bible speaks of, this could be a sort of representation or a sign, pointing to Jesus Christ of Nazareth, as the King of Kings and Lord of Lords, as He was born in Bethlehem, the city of David (Matt. 2:1). This gate city of Bethlehem, may be representative of, entering the city, where Jesus Christ Immanuel of Nazareth was born, into this world, to save us from our sins (Isa. 7:14, Matt. 1:21, 23)! Just another confirmation that Jesus Christ of Nazareth is indeed and always will be "…Wonderful, Counselor, The mighty God, The everlasting Father, The Prince of Peace…" (Isa. 9:6). It should be said, that other places in the Bible name Jerusalem as the city where God dwells; but Bethlehem is very close to Jerusalem, and could easily be considered a "suburb" in modern day terms. Taking this into consideration, would maintain the continuity of Scriptural authority on the subject.

However, we must still always consider that God dwells in us, and with us (1 Cor. 3:16). In the book of Revelation account of the New Jerusalem; God is the tabernacle, in this life, we are His ultimate tabernacle and He is ours (1 Cor. 3:16, Rev. 21). This is the incredibly intimate and close relationship God desires, through Jesus Christ of Nazareth, God, the Father's, only begotten Son, with each and every one of us, through His Holy Spirit (Ps. 46:11, John 17:22, 23)! Ezekiel 36 in particular, is a wonderful depiction of God's future intent for all of the descendants of the house of Israel. It is hard to argue that God's people, each and every one of us, have not disobeyed Him at one point in time or another in our life. But Ezekiel 36 speaks of restoration of both, the land and the spirit (Ezek. 36:24-28)! God has always planned for us to dwell in peace and abundance; it is His way (Gen. 1:31, Ezek. 36:35)! It is our own desires and selfishness, that have caused us to actually reject God's blessings, if you can believe it (Isa. 59:2)! That being said, this prophecy is undoubtedly already taking place; but has likely, a much greater fulfillment in the future, for the house of Israel, and all of mankind, in general (Gen. 22:18, 28:14).

Now, Zechariah 14 talks about the Lord standing on the mount of Olives with "…his feet…" and the mount shall cleave from the east and to the west, half of the mountain will move north and half will move south and "…living waters…" will come out of it, half to the hinder, Mediterranean sea, and half to the former, Dead sea (Zech. 14:4-8). There are a couple points to mention about this subject; first, is that Jesus did indeed stand on the Mount of Olives, and prophesied there and spent time there before His betrayal (Matt. 24, 26:30). But in all accounts, the mount did not cleave and issue out "…living waters…" literally, albeit, Jesus is the "…living water…" (Zech. 14:8, John 7:38, 39). Now comes the "spiritual" context; Ezekiel 11:23, says "…the glory of the LORD…stood…" on the mount on the east of the city, likely the Mount of Olives; so if Jesus were to stand on the mount again and it were to cleave literally, it may be that His Holy Spirit or His glory is present (Gen. 49:10, Isa. 2:2). And the second point is, in reference to the waters; the first reference is mentioned in Ezekiel 47:1-12, that in the "Messianic Age", a temple will be built, with the possibility of literal water flowing out of it towards the east, and used as healing; possibly to heal the Dead sea of its high salt concentration. The other water spoken of going toward the Mediterranean may be literal; but it is more likely a Spiritual reference to Jesus Christ of Nazareth, God, the Father, and His Holy Spirit being the "…living waters…"; as well as those whom will be travelling to Jerusalem to worship God, coming from, amongst other places, the west, as much of the west has Judeo-Christian roots in our ancestry (Prov. 18:4, Isa. 2:2, 33:20-24, Jer. 17:13, John 4:10). This interpretation may reconcile the literal and spiritual relationship of this verse with other verses on the subject in the Bible.

Last, we must always remember that the Bible is a book that speaks about physical things, that actually take place here on earth, but the Bible also has a "Spiritual" perspective. We as human beings, are made up of the dust, our spirit, and our soul; we must also read the Bible, as referencing both the natural and the spiritual realm (Eccl. 12:7, Mal. 2:15, Matt. 5:28, 10:28). This can be a challenge at times, and takes patience to understand all that God may be saying to us through the Bible, but that is what draws us closer to Him every day; and it also gives us the opportunity to fellowship with others and speak about our ideas, interpretations and questions, of what the Bible says. The Bible and its teachings; ultimately bring life and fellowship, both with God and humankind together in His Holy Spirit, through God, the Father's, only begotten Son, Jesus Christ of Nazareth. Alleluia and praise the LORD. Amen and Amen.

Restructuring

Right education is the key (Hos. 4:6). Some form of the creation account, in place of evolutionary theory, may be taught in most, if not all schools. Evolutionary theory, in general, may be removed, and replaced with God's account of creation, such as the 7 day account of creation, with Adam and Eve, as our earthly ancestral, father and mother. DNA evidence, apparently, has already proven with some high percent of accuracy that we all came from one man and one woman! Also, the flood account may be accepted rather than the stratification theory of millions of years of the earth's development, using the earth's crust (Gen. 7). And the development of languages of nations, cultures and boundaries, based on Biblical understanding of the disbursement of peoples and nations, rather than what is currently taught in schools may be reinforced (Gen. 10:25, 11:1-9). And last, the idea that dinosaurs are millions of years old may also be considered nonsense (Job 40:15-24). If you believe what the Bible says, there is no room for doubt, God said He created it all, and He did it "...suddenly..." (Isa. 48:3). Where is the room for evolutionary theory? More will be talked about of these ideas, in another book; but there are many websites and organization that can be found on the internet substantiating the Creation account of this world's history, rather than the so called "evolutionary" theory. Evolutionary theory, no doubt, is a direct result of Adam and Eve's disobedience to God, when they chose to eat from the fruit of the tree of knowledge of good and evil (Gen. 3:22).

As said above, one of the major moves of restructuring would be to the education system, and the change in nature of the many "professions" that we currently have in the early 21st century A.D.. Think of a world without any major physical or mental illness. There is quite a long list of professions that would not likely be needed, at least in the same capacity they are as of the early 21st century A.D., including all of the "offshoot" businesses and jobs, that are involved in the various industries, the health "industry" being the most prominent one! Of course, we have always had "alternative" methods to "curing" diseases; but the point is, if we lived in a world which did not have them, at least, in the magnitude and severity we see them in the early 21st century A.D., then the economic and governing structures that support this current system, would go through a change to say the least. Not to say that doctors and other "health" professionals would not be needed, out right; but that the way in which they practice could very well change according to the health concerns of the possible "Messianic Age" needs. Regarding language, in particular, some have suggested that all will be speaking one language based on Zephaniah 3:9; which would certainly remove the language barriers from this current world, and make it much easier to fellowship, teach and conduct business; but it is possible, that this verse is referring to the "purity" of our conversation rather than the actual language that we speak (Ps. 12:6, Eph. 4:29). Because the next question would inevitably be, what language would we all speak; Hebrew, English, French, etc.? Only time will tell the truth of the fulfillment of this prophetic verse.

Another consideration is the change in land distribution and allotment. The first obvious change regarding land, is in the land of Israel. In Ezekiel 48, it explains the boundaries of

Israel extending north of and bordering Damascus, which is in Syria, and also includes the boundaries of Lebanon. You can see appendix D, for a pictorial map of these proposed boundaries. There are many other prophecies in the Old Testament, that speak of Israel being given these lands again, where their ancient ancestors once lived in and still do today; as much of these lands continue to be inhabited or re-inhabited by the descendants of Israel (Jer. 30, 31; Obad. 19-21). Nevertheless, as Jew and Gentile believers in Christ, we have first and foremost a heavenly home to aim for (Phil. 3:20, John 18:36). Prophecy will be fulfilled here on earth, and if this interpretation is literal, then there is, no doubt, that there will be Christ followers living in Israel during the "Messianic Age", as there are already. But we have a better hope, and a better promise, than these earthly vessels, we currently dwell in (Heb. 11:16, John 14:2, 3). There is also a general promise, that land will be distributed equitably to all. It says that, "…they shall sit every man under his vine…" (Mic. 4:4). This could also be referencing Jesus, as He was and is the "…true vine…" (John 15:1). But there must be something to this on a physical level, in that, people will likely have their own land space to enjoy!

Along the same "theme" as land allotment, is the land reformation. The massive and multiple earthquakes, that are said to take place during the "Great Tribulation", will likely alter, to say the least, much of earth's topography (Matt. 24:7, Luke 21:11, Rev. 6:12, 8:5, 11:13, 19, 16:18). It is said that mountains are going to move, and possibly crumble, and islands are going to flee away (Isa. 40:4, Ezek. 38:20, Rev. 16:20). This may change vast landscapes around the earth, and possibly where much of the major mountain ranges exist as of the early 21st century A.D., such as the Himalayas, Rockies, etc. (Ps. 46:2, 6). Some of this was fulfilled "spiritually" in John the Baptist's preaching, and it has been said that mountains can be referring to the governments or authorities; but there is still likely a future context to this, on a greater more physical scale (Luke 3:4, 5). Only time will tell what the truth of this is; but the fact is, that what God says, will be done (Ps. 114:7, Jud. 5:5, and Nah. 1:5). Zechariah 14 speaks candidly about a portion of these earthquakes and the results of them; namely, that "…living waters…" stream from a split in the earth's crust at Jerusalem, as mentioned earlier (Ps. 46:3, 4; Zech. 14:8). These same waters are spoken of in Ezekiel 47:1-12; as I have described in greater detail a possible interpretation of this prophecy, in the previous section of this chapter, and in other areas of this book. Along with this idea of land reformation, is the idea of the Jerusalem temple worship centre being restored (Ezek. 40-46). See chapter five for more, about a possible future physical temple in Jerusalem.

Another concept, which has already had a resurgence today, is Biblical agricultural practices, one of which, being that the land receives rest every seventh year (Lev. 25:4). This is for the land to replenish its nutrients; it gives the animals, plants and the human workers, rest, as well. The other purpose, is to keep in mind those, whom are less fortunate, whom are able to glean food from the land during this time, in orchards, etc. (Lev. 25:6, 7). Which is another Biblical agricultural practice, not harvesting the corners of the fields, the corners are to be left for those whom could use them; travellers, the poor, etc. (Lev. 19:9, 10, 23:22; Deut. 24:19). Other ideas that are resurging in the early 21st century A.D., are the concepts of organic growing methods, rather than using industry made fertilizers and pesticides. There are continuous arguments on this subject, as current practices are said to degrade soil quality, and produce an inferior quality product. Natural methods of agriculture only stand to reason, but often "efficient" production, economics and human demand in this age seem to require higher yields, possibly at the expense of our own health and the health of the earth's environment, only time will tell. I know from personal experience that giving the land rest works, as I have had more than enough produce to last the two years that I let the land "rest" in a garden I was growing. Of course, you need to sow, harvest and preserve the food in the sixth year, but God does not expect us to just sit back and do nothing in this life (Prov. 6:6). This is very similar to the concept of the manna in the wilderness; God provided the extra manna on the sixth day, to be collected to provide for food, during the day of rest, the seventh day Sabbath (Ex. 16:22-26). And then the remaining was to be disposed of, after that. The point is, if we obey God, He provides and gives us more than we need!

Last, in Ezekiel 39, Isaiah 2:4 and Micah 4:3; the prophets speak of a time where weapons will be beaten into plowshares and nations will not rise up to war against other nations anymore, as I had mentioned briefly earlier. Of course, we are not currently at that point in human history, as of the early 21st century A.D., at least not mankind collectively; so this is also, at least partly, a future promise. Although there are nations in this world that do currently see relative peace today; this promise is likely to extend to all of earth's inhabitants during the so called "Messianic Age". Ezekiel 39 goes into greater detail of burning weapons and "…burying…" the dead, as the majority of this will likely take place after the "Great Tribulation", but never the less, as is mentioned in my book, "Time, Times and a Dividing of Time – What did John really see?", this will be a necessary job during the "aftermath" and outset of the "Millennial reign of Christ with His saints", as I had mentioned earlier. Regarding peace; Isaiah 19:23-25 says, "In that day shall there be a highway out of Egypt to Assyria, and the Assyrian shall come into Egypt, and the Egyptian into Assyria, and the Egyptians shall serve with the Assyrians. In that day shall Israel be the third with Egypt and with Assyria, *even* a blessing in the midst of the land: Whom the LORD of hosts shall bless, saying, Blessed *be* Egypt my people, and Assyria the work of my hands, and Israel mine inheritance.". Assyria likely meaning Syria and some of its cohorts today; what a wonderful time we have to look forward to! That being said, no doubt, we can still experience and are experiencing a portion of this prophecy being fulfilled today! But the future, ultimately, is bright! With God, the Father, Jesus Christ of Nazareth, God's only begotten Son, and His Holy Spirit; we are more than conquerors (Rom. 8:37)!

Redistributing

Redistribution is and has already been happening, from colonization over the millennia; and especially since the "Great Commission" was first given by Jesus Christ of Nazareth, to "…teach all nations…to observe all things whatsoever…" He has commanded us (Matt. 24:14, 28:16-20). This is being done, through teaching natives how to develop a better quality of life standard, including best sanitation practices and food growing methods, and was prophesied to happen thousands of years ago, through the blessings of Abraham's obedience to God (Gen. 22:18). It is also being done, through mission trips from Churches, Non-Governmental Organizations, and other governing bodies, as well; such as the UN. These are all great, but again, in this world's present condition, we still have much more to accomplish to bring equality to the four corners of the earth. Again, right education is the key (Hos. 4:6). That being said, as has been mentioned before; we cannot force methods, ideas or ethical ways on other nations, peoples and tongues around us (John 6:44, Rev. 17:14). Jesus came to serve, not to be a tyrant, and He calls us friends, not slaves (Matt. 20:28, John 15:15, Gal. 4:7). This is how we need to reach out to others, with the love of God in Jesus Christ of Nazareth, first and foremost, in our mind and heart (John 13:34). Any other motive would be selfish and unfruitful in the end (Jam. 4:3). Jesus desires us to bear fruit for Him and His kingdom; this is why He came, to save all of mankind, not for material gain, which is a result of following God, but so that we can receive eternal life in God's kingdom, through Jesus Christ of Nazareth (Matt. 6:33, 19:29; John 3:16, 17). Alleluia and praise the LORD. Amen and Amen.

Speaking of "tithing" in particular; God makes very clear what is wrong with the world today. In Malachi, He speaks of our disobedience in neglecting to pay our tithe to Him. Malachi 3:10 says, "Bring ye all the tithes into the storehouse…". In Malachi 3:7 and 8 it says, "…Wherein shall we return?" and God says, "Will a man rob God? Yet ye have robbed me. But ye say, Wherein have we robbed thee? In tithes and offerings.". Although it is a challenge to choose one place to tithe to, in the early 21st century A.D. world, as there are many different religious denominations and charitable organizations. Not to mention the portion we pay to the government from our income, which Jesus spoke about, "…Render to Caesar the things that are Caesar's, and to God the things that are God's." (Mark 12:17). This is where cheerful giving comes in to play, not doing it out of compulsion or grudgingly (2 Cor. 9:7). He also spoke of reconciling with our brothers and/or sisters first, before we offer our gifts at the altar; if they have something against us (Matt. 5:23, 24)! So, the future temple will likely accept the tithes from all nations; although it is possible that the people of Israel proper will be able to provide for the offerings in the temple throughout the year. This temple will likely be for all of the inhabitants of the earth to enjoy, with the inner court, likely being set aside for the Levites (Ezra 6:8-10, Ezek. 44:15-17). See chapter five and appendix G for more information on this future prospective temple and its details. Nonetheless, more important than an actual physical tithe, is the fact that the act of tithing recognizes God as the main provider of all that we have in this world; as the Holy Bible of God says of God, "…for all things *come* of thee, and of thine own have we given thee." (1 Chr. 29:14).

There is an interesting description of the purpose of tithing, in relation to our blessings, as well as with the Feast of Booths, also known as the Feast of Tabernacles or "Sukkot", in the fall, and other annual Holy days (Deut. 16: 13-17). The Feast of Tabernacles is the fall feast, that was, and is attended to, by some as of the early 21st century A.D., that represents the ancient dwelling of the Israelites in the wilderness, Jesus Christ of Nazareth's dwelling with us, and is very likely the holyday that foreshadows the coming "Messianic Age" (Col. 2:17, Heb. 10:1). In these cases, the tithes were saved to literally be eaten at these festivals by those whom produced them (Deut. 12). There are other circumstances that could take place; like if the families were too far from the feast site, the harvest could be converted into money by selling it, like market farms, grocery stores and the restaurants of today do, and then use the money to buy and eat at the site or even stay and eat within their own gates (Deut. 12:21, Deut. 14:22-27)! This allowance may have been more associated with the spring holydays, such as Passover, with the feast of unleavened bread and the feast of weeks, also known as Pentecost, seven weeks after the first Sabbath, after Passover, only; or all feast days, it is challenging for me to say (Lev. 23:4-21). This subject may be spoken of in greater detail in another book, but most importantly, is to note, that God does indeed have a plan for mankind, and that includes particular days, and weeks set aside, for a sign, to remind us of our past trials with God, our present blessings, and future promises! Aside from the tithing commandment, that brings us to all of these representative days and weeks, these holydays give us a chance to rest, replenish and worship our Creator! Which was His plan from the beginning, in the commandment, "Six days shalt thou labour, and do all thy work: But the seventh day *is* the sabbath of the LORD thy God..." (Gen. 2:1-3, Ex. 20:8-11).

Also, these spring holydays are where the Christian "Easter" and "Pentecost" equivalent of "mainstream" Christianity come from, as Jesus was crucified and buried on the Passover, and the Feast of Unleavened bread proceeded it the next seven days, Jesus arising the third day after Passover, in the midst of the feast of unleavened bread, and He revealed Himself on the first day of the week, seven weeks before Pentecost, and His Holy Spirit was poured out on Pentecost (John 19:31, Acts 2)! Although these Biblical dates are not always celebrated at exactly the same time, as traditional "Easter" as of the early 21st century A.D., for some reasons mentioned, including Adam and Eve and Israel's rebellion against God, they are still indeed related (Gen. 3:22, 1 Kings 11, 12)! At any rate, these tithes were literally for the people whom laboured to produce them, as God blessed them with the fruits of their labour, as well as blessing, of course, their children, the Levite with them, that is, our priest, minister or pastor equivalent, and the hired help whom helped bring forth the harvest (Deut. 12:18)! Deuteronomy 16:16 and 17 simplify all of this, they say, "Three times in a year shall all thy males appear before the LORD thy God in the place which he shall choose; in the feast of unleavened bread, and in the feast of weeks, and in the feast of tabernacles: and they shall not appear before the LORD empty: Every man *shall give* as he is able, according to the blessing of the LORD thy God which he hath given thee.". Although all of these "feasts" may be kept by many or all in the "Messianic Age", the Feast of Tabernacles seems to be the obvious and most important one mentioned in Zechariah 14:16-20. I can only imagine, that not every person would likely go up to Jerusalem from every nation each year, but possibly a "delegate" family from each nation, may go up. Let common sense and God's Spiritual wisdom prevail in the truth of all of this!

However, regarding the Feast of Tabernacles, think of it like the "thanksgiving" holiday that is celebrated annually today, at least in the West. In the end, the point is, that we can develop a "negative" idea about tithing sometimes, like the idea somebody is taking "my" money or supply. But in actual fact, the tithe is not only for God, but for us! This becomes particularly obvious in the likely use of the "Messianic Age", which is to bring the tithes in for the priests to "offer", cook and then be eaten, likely by the very people who brought them in, along with the Levites, those in need and God as required! See chapter five for more detail on the topic of the "Messianic Age" Temple. It is clear today that the "who" and "what" of tithing can be a confusing topic at times, but as the New Testament says, give with a cheerful heart, not grudgingly (2 Cor. 9:7). This should keep the ideas, rules, etc., of tithing, simple; as the truth is revealed to each of us of what we are to do with our "increase" and blessings. Letting God's Holy Spirit guide us in giving, is always a good start! Also, more will be spoken about the topic of the Feast of Tabernacles in the next two chapters.

One last topic to discuss regarding re-distribution should be considered, namely the skills and blessings that were prophesied to be given to the 12 tribes of Israel and their descendants (Gen. 49, Deut. 33, etc.). Each of these tribes were given certain gifts and abilities, that will in all likelihood come into play, in the future, regarding; rebuilding, restructuring and redistributing. God has also given each of us, as individuals, certain talents or gifts (1 Cor. 12). As the Bible says, "But now *are they* many members, yet but one body." (1 Cor. 12:20). We all have our particular strengths and weaknesses (2 Cor. 12:9). It is through these gifts, that we have been given, as individuals and nations; that we can best serve God and mankind. So when the time comes, no doubt God will have prepared each person or nation of people for their specific tasks in this "Messianic Age" (Eph. 2:10). Namely, we must obey God and Him only, worship Him, listen to Him and to His authority through whom He gives it; in order to determine our "jobs", "tasks", "careers", etc., in this life. All for God's glory of course! And for our benefit as members of the body of Christ until our final day here on earth, and forever more in Jesus Christ of Nazareth's Holy name, Amen (Eccl. 2:24, 25, 3:22, 5:19, 8:15)!

Conclusion

The three "R's" are a good and simple way of looking at "starting over"; but the most important thing to remember, is that God's kingdom is spiritual in nature, first and foremost (1 Cor. 15:50). God was before we were, He is "...I AM..."; He is the existing one, Jehovah; the very nature of God is everlasting (Ex. 3:14, Job 36:26, Ps. 102:12, John 8:58). Jesus said of Himself, "Heaven and earth shall pass away, but my words shall not pass away." (Matt. 24:35). The point is, that whatever is to happen here on earth in the future, for ourselves, our families and descendants forever; God desires us to seek His kingdom, and righteousness, first and foremost (Matt. 6:33)! This kingdom can be "experienced" in the natural realm when we have rest, peace, justice, abundance, love, joy, etc. (Isa. 32:16-18). The fruit of the Holy Spirit are manifestations of God's kingdom in us (Gal. 5:22, 23). God is a Spirit, and His Kingdom is spiritual, first and foremost (Matt. 12:28, John 4:24, Rom. 14:17, 18). He created the natural realm for His glory, and so that we can learn to share in His glory, and His eternal kingdom, with Him forever! As the Bible says, "Now this I say, brethren, that flesh and blood cannot inherit the kingdom of God..." (1 Cor. 15:50).

Even if the "Messianic Age" is to be literal, I think that we as human beings would still go about our business, possibly with more purpose in mind (Col. 3:17, 23; Eph. 6:7)! The purpose being, that God is preparing each of us for eternity and that earthly gain, is not really the final goal (John 14:3, 18:36; Phil. 1:21). Even today there is much "phraseology" in the culture regarding this "Messianic age", there are the "millennials" referring to an age group, many different structures and technology have the "millennial" name tagged to them. Of course, much of this has to do with the beginning of the 21st century, but the point is, that the "Millennial spirit" is lingering large, as of the early 21st century A.D.. This is where the fruit of the spirit, "... longsuffering..." comes into play (Gal. 5:22). No man knows when exactly Christ is "coming", or when this "Messianic Age" is going to start, but Jesus said to watch and pray (Luke 21:36). So all we can do, today, is follow God's Holy Spirit, obey God, and if we have not yet; start a relationship with God, through Jesus Christ of Nazareth, God's only begotten Son, and except His Holy Spirit into our life; mind, body and soul (Luke 11:13, 1 Cor. 2:14, Heb. 4:12). Patience is the key, as the Holy Bible says, "In your patience possess ye your souls." (Luke 21:19).

It is good to have an enthusiastic attitude, but what is most important, is to be obedient to God. As I had mentioned in an earlier book, no need to be a "hero" when one is not called for (1 Thess. 4:11). God will prepare and is preparing each and every one of us, for our part on this side of the "Messianic Age", for either being a part of it and its rebuilding, or for preparing the next generation for it. This has been the same since the beginning of time; the children of God have a responsibility to the "next" generation, to pass on; knowledge, wisdom and the truth of God, so that the "torch" continues to burn. Running the race, until Jesus does finally return to take us home where He is (John 14:3, Heb. 12:1, 2)!

Discussion: The Order of the "Messianic Age"

"To love rightly is to love what is orderly and beautiful
in an educated and disciplined way."
– Plato

A lot has been said in this chapter and there is a lot to digest. As the old saying goes, "Rome was not built in a day". Well the fact of the matter is, this world has not come to this point overnight. We have been building, growing, waring, dying and rebuilding for close to 6000 years, as of the early 21st century A.D.. As we approach the possibility of the dawn of a "Messianic Age", we need to take our time, especially if there are some events that are to come upon this world before it, that will likely shake the earth, like this world has never experienced before, and never will experience again (Matt. 24:21). God is a God of order and decency, we need to follow His lead and do the same (1 Cor. 14:33, 40). This may require repentance on our part, tossing out old ideas that are either complete lies, or are no longer "valid". We need to be thinking about what changes we need to make in our daily, weekly and yearly "routine" and we also need to reconsider our relationship with our Maker and others (Hag. 1:7)! This will not happen overnight, but it took six evenings and mornings to create the earth and all that is in it with God resting on the seventh day, so we also likely have some time (Gen. 1:31-2:3)!

Discussion Questions

1. What types of changes to this world's health system and the way it views patient care might need to take place in order to provide effectively for a world that no longer has major "illnesses", physical or mental, plaguing it any longer? What about other infrastructure systems?

   _____

   _____

   _____

2. Does God really like order? How about a proper education system? What can we do about it?

   _____

   _____

   _____

3. Imagining a time when all people are at some sort of agreement on religious issues. It may sound like a "pipe dream" in the world we live in, as of the early 21st century A.D., but it seems God will bring something like this about. What can we do in the meantime while we are waiting or "working" towards this goal of peace on earth?

   _____

   _____

   _____

CHAPTER 4

GOD'S GOVERNMENT IN THE "MESSIANIC AGE"

"He shall cause them that come of Jacob to take root: Israel shall blossom and bud, and fill the face of the world with fruit."

— ISAIAH 27:6

Introduction

I have read a fair amount about the Kingdom of God on earth, and what it will look like from a governing perspective. Three things are apparent and obvious; God will be in control, His Holy Spirit will be sovereign, and the knowledge of the Lord will not need to be taught like it is in the early 21st century A.D.. Because everyone will know Him, and everyone will worship Him; especially at the Feast of Tabernacles, or their nation will be punished (Zech. 14:16-19). There could be a few reasons why everyone will know whom God is; but I am sure it is related to Jesus' prophecy of the "...gospel..." being preached to all nations and then the "...end..." coming (Matt. 24:14). The end likely meaning the end of the age, the "Great Tribulation" and then the "Millennial reign of Christ with His saints"; the "Great Tribulation" being another testimony to mankind that God's Word is truth and will be fulfilled, like the flood was in Noah's day (Matt. 24:21, 37; 28:20).

There are multiple verses that speak of there being an outpouring of God's Holy Spirit in the "...last days..." (Joel 2:28, Hab. 2:14, Acts 2:17). This was partially fulfilled in Jesus' earthly ministry, crucifixion, burial and resurrection three days later, with the outpouring of God's Holy Spirit on Pentecost, fifty days later (Acts 2:17). But it still continues today until the entire world knows the true God (Matt. 24:14, Rom. 14:11). The keeping of the Feast of Tabernacles, is just one of the commanded feasts of God, which can be found in Leviticus 23; of which, most were briefly mentioned, in the previous chapter. They are not kept by all today, because of various reasons; one being that the tribes of Israel turned from God thousands of years ago, as mentioned earlier; but also because God is likely looking to reach mankind with a more simple lesson at present. Because not all mankind are necessarily Israelites, and the message of Jesus Christ of Nazareth and His life is the simplest method of putting forth the "Good news", that is, there is a resurrection of the body and soul and that we can have eternal life in Jesus' Holy name (John 3:14, 15; 1 Cor. 15:42,1 John 5:11-13). However, Jesus did keep the Hebrew feasts with His family (Matt. 26:17, John 7:37)!

Nevertheless, the Bible focuses on us receiving and being led by the Holy Spirit, first and foremost (John 3:5, Acts 1:8, Rom. 8:26). This was Jesus' last message, before ascending to heaven, that the Holy Spirit was being sent, and that we should not blaspheme the Holy Spirit, mainly because it is the Spirit of life, but also because it is the spirit that is to guide us, teach us and nurture us (John 3:6-8, 6:63, 14:15-17, Rom. 8:6). This Spirit is the spirit that dwells in His true believers and organizes us, as the Body of Christ (Rom. 8:9, Eph. 2:22). In Ezekiel 36:26 it says, "A new heart also will I give you, and a new spirit will I put within you…". And in 1 Timothy 6:16 it says of God, "Who only hath immortality, **dwelling in the light which no man can approach unto; whom no man hath seen, nor can see**: to whom *be* honour and power everlasting. Amen.". The point is, that God in His fullness is a very bright light. It is His Holy Spirit that has been given to mediate between Himself and mankind today, and likely until the "…end…", but Jesus Christ of Nazareth, God, the Father's, only begotten Son, is with us through His Holy Spirit, forever (Matt. 28:20; John 14:16)! As the Bible says of Jesus, "For where two or three are gathered together in my name, there am I in the midst of them." (Matt. 18:20).

The Lord's coming Kingdom and His saints

Many references to the coming of the Lord, and His saints or angels, are mentioned in the Bible. And some include references to experiences that have already taken place (Ex. 12:23, 19:11; Num. 23:3, 1 Sa. 10:6, Deut. 33:2, Zech. 12:10, John 19:37). That being said, to say that He is not "coming again" would be sacrilegious, to say the least. God, Christ and those inspired by His Holy Spirit, to write the New and Old Testaments; spoke of an age, whether it be spiritual, physical or both, that would be ruled by the Sovereign Lord; God, the Father, and Jesus Christ of Nazareth, God's only begotten Son, through His Holy Spirit with His Host (Rev. 20:4, 6). That being said, there are also prophecies of similar descriptions that may describe the very end of earth's present history as a whole, and the "…new heavens and a new earth…", but that will be spoken of in another book (2 Pet. 3:13). This "…end…" of earth's present history, the final "judgement", and the "…new heavens and a new earth…"; are spoken of in various places in the Holy Bible, for the interested reader (Isa. 66:15, 2 Pet. 3:10-13, Jude 1:15, Rev. 20:7-15, 21, 22, etc.).

The Old Testament scriptures say of Jesus, that "…they shall look upon me whom they have pierced…" (Zech. 12:10). This was fulfilled in Christ on the cross, the "crucifixes" and crosses of the early 21ˢᵗ century A.D., may also be a testimony to it, although some may consider them idols; they can still be used as visual representation and testimony to the belief of Jesus Christ of Nazareth and His sacrifice for us (John 19:37). The later portion of this fulfillment, especially in Revelation 1:7, is likely the Spirit of grace (Zech. 12:10). This is the period of time we are in, in the early 21ˢᵗ century A.D., until the gospel message has been preached unto the nations and the "..end…" comes; namely, the "Great Tribulation", and then the "Messianic Age", I am speaking of in this book, if indeed it is to be literal (Matt. 24:13). However, there might also be a connection of this "concept" with the very end of this earth's present history, at the final judgement (Dan. 7:9-14, Rev. 1:7, 20:11-15). The point is, that God places more than enough evidence in front of us, to believe in Jesus Christ, and follow Him, in this life. If we deny Him, that is something that will have to be dealt with on the day of judgement (Rev. 20:11-15). Nevertheless, it is not the purpose of this book to speak of God's final judgement.

As far as their likeness goes, there is much reference to what a saint or a resurrected being will be like in the "spiritual" Kingdom of God (Phil. 1:19). Mostly, it refers to them being like the angels of heaven (Ps. 90:10, Matt. 16:27, 22:30, 25:31; Luke 20:36, 2 Thess. 1:7). Even the apostles speculated and were not sure what they would be like, when they were resurrected; but they knew that they would be like Christ (1 Cor. 15:51, 52; 1 John 3:2). And the Bible does hint at their general location, especially at the very end of this earth's present history (Isa. 33:20-24, Rev. 5:9-10, 20:9). The transfiguration of Christ, when Moses and Elijah were revealed, might be a hint to where the saints are, as well (Matt. 17:1-13). Not to mention, that the New Testament spoke about "…many…of the saints…" being resurrected at Jesus' resurrection and being seen in the city (Matt. 27:52, 53). The point is, that God's kingdom is much more than we can fathom (Isa. 55:9). And that will go with how the resurrected saints and Jesus, "manifest" themselves, during the time often referred to as the "Messianic Age". However, if you have a relationship with Jesus today, I think that will give you a pretty good idea, about how a relationship with Jesus, and the saints for that matter, would be like in the "Messianic Age"; if we are heading towards one here on earth, as of the early 21ˢᵗ century A.D.!

Man's rule and government

One of the first commands God gave Adam, was for man to have dominion over the earth (Gen. 1:28). Why would God go back on His word (Num. 23:19)? There is also the promise in Isaiah, that God's Word would not depart from the mouths of His people and their descendants after them (Isa. 59:2). In the book of Numbers, it describes the whole nation of Israel, as if God had "…not beheld iniquity in Jacob, neither hath he seen perverseness in Israel…" (Num. 23:21). The point is, that God's people, Israel, the 12 tribes and their descendants, although turning to idolatry from time to time, are still God's people! The saints and Jesus Christ of Nazareth are only the "…firstfruits…" of all of God's creation (Jam. 1:18). We, as men and women, still need to live out our lives here on earth, following God; regardless of whether or not we are "called" or "chosen" to be saints in this life, the next or any other after that (Ps. 115:16). Hebrews 2:5 says, "For unto the angels hath he not put in subjection the world to come, whereof we speak.". Is this not proof enough that the "...angels spirits..." will not be "in charge" of the world to come, or possibly even the "Messianic Age" (Ps. 104:4)?

Moses was taught by his father in law, about governing structures, whom was not an Israelite (Ex. 18). In Isaiah, it speaks of the kings of the earth ministering and supporting Jerusalem and its people (Isa. 60:3, 10)! Proverbs says that, "The king's heart *is* in the hand of the LORD..." (Prov. 21:1). And in Jeremiah and elsewhere, it says, "...that the way of man *is* not in himself..." (Ps. 37:23, Prov. 20:24, Jer. 10:23). Even Nebuchadnezzar, a king of Babylon, recognized and submitted to the supremacy of God, although he had to experience some trials to submit (Dan. 4:37)! Not to mention, the fact, that God has already prepared man's "...good works..." for him ahead of time (Eccl. 3:11, Eph. 2:10)! And in Romans 2, it speaks of the Gentiles being "...a law unto themselves...Which shew the work of the law written in their hearts..." (Rom. 2:14, 15). The point is, God is sovereign, and He rules man on some level, saint or not, wither we realize it or not! Praise the Lord, God Almighty, Creator of the Heavens and the Earth and all that are in them!

As far as human representatives of God are concerned, the Priesthood, at the temple, will be a physical manifestation of God's sovereignty (Ezek. 44:24). They will be administering the law, and will be "judges" over the people, possibly something like the legal system of today; that is, if there will indeed be a literal "Messianic Age" or "Millennial reign of Christ with His saints" (Isa. 1:26, 27). And the "prince" will be something of a representative for God and the people, as well (Jer. 30:21, Ezek. 45:16, 22). In Zechariah 12:8 it says, the House of David will be "...as God...as the angel of the Lord...". Also Jeremiah's prophesy would suggest that kings and princes, plural; would come to Jerusalem "...sitting on the throne of David..." (Jer. 17:25, 26). This would suggest that David's paternal lineage remains on earth today! And whether it is David's lineage, that maintains the throne, or another tribe; it is important to remember that Jesus has the title of "...King of Kings..." and "...Lord of Lords...", forever (Gen. 49:10, Jer. 31:9, Ps. 108:8, 1 Cor. 12:12, Rom. 4:16, 10:6-8, Deut. 30:11-14, 1 Tim. 6:15, Rev. 19:16). Also, if or when the earthly "authority" changes tribal hands, it is likely that the paternal lineage of David's descendants may still maintain their status; as the Bible says in numerous places, that we can all be a nation of kings and priests in Christ Jesus of Nazareth (Ex. 19:6, 1 Pet. 2:9, Rev. 1:6, 5:10).

Last, in Jeremiah 30, it does speak of "...nobles..." and a "...governor.." coming from Israel or "...Jacob's tents...", the descendants of the 12 tribes of Israel (Jer. 30:18, 21). This is more general in nature, which will give some "leeway" to those whom are going to be a part of this prophecy, on the "who's who" of the truth of this prophecy; but regardless, God calls people, He establishes authorities, and He will do the same in the "Messianic Age" (Rom. 13:1). There is no need to be anxious or worry about that (Phil. 4:6). Verse 24 confirms the timing of this prophecy, as it says, in the "…latter days ye shall consider it." (Jer. 30:24). These are the "…latter days…" or "…last days…", spoken of throughout the Bible, that we are currently in today (Isa. 2:2-4, Mic. 4:1-3, 2 Tim. 3:1)! This time has continued from the time of Jesus Christ of Nazareth's earthly ministry, until now, and will continue. Jesus fulfilled ALL of the prophecies of being the "…King of Israel…", and He rules us whether we understand it, believe it, or not (Isa. 9:6-7, 11:1-9; Luke 2:11, Matt. 3:16, 28:18; John 1:49, 3:34, 7:24). But as I had mentioned many times previously, He works in and through us, to accomplish His work (Phil. 2:13). This is where the comparison of us, and the Church as a whole, to the "Body of Christ", is so important! He lives through us all! Glory be to God, the Father, Almighty!

The Body of Christ

Putting some Old Testament and New Testament scriptures side by side, and comparing and "interpreting" them can bring some light to God's purpose for mankind; namely, His "body", the "body" of Christ, the "Church", "Congregation", of God, etc.. In Daniel 2:34 it speaks of a rock "hewn" not with man's hands. This is likely referring to Jesus, but when we look at Isaiah 51:1, which says, we were cut or "…hewn…" from a rock, as well; than the verse can be put into a more literal context. We have God, His Holy Spirit; God, the Body of Christ; and God, Jesus Christ Immanuel, and we are all One, in God, His Holy Spirit, through Jesus Christ of Nazareth, God, the Father's, only begotten Son (1 Cor. 12:12). This body of Christ is what I am pointing to, US, the "…people of God…" (Rom. 12:5, 1 Cor. 12:27, Heb. 4:9). The point is, that God made mankind to live on earth, and to have "…dominion…" over it (Gen. 1:26-28). I have heard that it is a sort of "testing" ground, for every one of us, for God to help prepare our mind, body and soul, for eternity (2 Cor. 4:17). We are God's children; He loves us and desires us to be like Him (John 3:16, Rom. 5:8, 8:29; 2 Cor. 3:18, Gal. 3:26, 1 John 2:6, 3:2)!

One thing is for certain, the law will go forth from Zion (Isa. 2:3). And men will almost certainly be following the Biblical commandments of God (John 4:23). However, God never intended for man to rule over man (1 Sam. 12:12-19). He always desired to be sovereign over all of us (Isa. 45:22, Zech. 1:3, Joel 2:12). Human ruler ship over each other is exactly that, a human devised concept (1 Sam. 12:12-19). God desires to be sovereign overall (Ps. 103:19, Dan. 4:17). And Jesus has authority and gives authority (Matt. 28:18-20). He desires to be our friend (John 15:15). Nevertheless, it was prophesied to Jacob by God, that kings would come from him (Gen. 35:11). Regarding following the Biblical commandments; we do, in general, have the "rule" of law in the early 21st century A.D., but Jesus came to show grace and save all of mankind, with one simple act; His death on the cross as a sinless man for the forgiveness of our sins, His burial, and His resurrection three days later, for a promise and a hope to all whom believe (Rom. 4:25). The Old Testament prophets speak about in various places, how God is not happy with how the people were or are following the "law"; He desires mercy, justice and righteousness, first and foremost (Isa. 1:11-20, Hos. 2:11, 19, 20). Jesus actually raised the bar from following the law carnally and literally, to follow it spiritually! He said if a man even looks at a woman lustfully, he has committed adultery with her, in his mind (Matt. 5:28). This is why the law must be bound on our mind and in our heart; because Jesus desires us to be like Him; sons and daughters of the living God (Jer. 31:33, Rom. 8:14, Col. 3:15, Heb. 8:10, 10:16; etc.). Of course, if man could not follow the physical law, how much harder would it be to follow it spiritually, well that is why we need God, Jesus Christ of Nazareth, God, the Father's, only begotten Son, and His Holy Spirit (Rom. 8:3-10). If we are following the Holy Spirit then the law of sin and death are not binding on us (Rom. 8:2, Gal. 5:16, 25).

So, this following of the law, does not negate the existence of Jesus Christ of Nazareth and His sacrifice. He was, is and is to come (Rev. 1:8, 4:8). Christ is the fulfilment of the law, if we were to follow the law perfectly, we would be like Jesus Christ of Nazareth; but because Jesus is a part of that law, we need Him to live, but we are justified by faith in Him, so the law of Christ is fulfilled by our faith in Jesus Christ of Nazareth, which is a gift from God (Matt. 5:17, Rom. 10:4, Gal. 3:24, 6:2; Eph. 2:8)! The point is, that Christ's Holy Spirit will flow from Zion and unto all of mankind (Joel 2:28). Again, this has already been fulfilled in the outpouring of the Holy Spirit on Pentecost, after Christ's resurrection in the early first century A.D., but will likely have a greater fulfillment in the "Messianic Age"; if there is to be a literal 1000 years of Christ reign with His saints (Acts 2:17, 18; Rev. 20:6). The Holy Spirit and God's ways will in all likelihood be a beacon of light to the world, flowing from Jerusalem, and Israel, in general, during the millennium and need not be any different today (Isa. 30:17)! Let's be honest, Jerusalem is where Christ spent much of His time in ministry; He was crucified just outside the gates there, He was buried just outside the gates and He arose from His garden tomb, just outside the northern gates of Jerusalem (Matt. 27:32-28:9). This city, Jerusalem, is special; there is no doubt about that. Its very name has the word "peace" in it, "shalom"; and can mean "to flow as water" of peace or "teach" of peace; Strong's numbers 3389 and 7999, respectively (Jos. 10:1, Ps. 25:8, Prov. 11:25, 16:17; Hos. 10:12). That being said, we should not ignore the "heavenly" or New Jerusalem that exists, wherever we are here on earth, and for eternity and is still yet to come (Rev. 21:2)!

What will these resurrected saints experience in the "Messianic Age"?

The saints are set apart and have been chosen by God throughout history, to experience and be given certain gifts and responsibilities, that are unlike others; just think of some of the saints of the Bible, such as; David, Joseph, Noah, the apostles, Jesus, etc.. This is why they are considered the "…firstfruits…" of God (Jam. 1:18). They are a chosen people, a "…royal priesthood…" (1 Pet. 2:9). They may very likely be "spiritually" with the men and women whom are governing the lands, through God's divine guidance, in the "Messianic Age" (Ps. 90:10, Prov. 21:1, Eccl. 12:7, Rom. 13:6, 2 Thess. 1:10). They may be revealed to some, and may not be (Heb. 13:2). Nevertheless, we are all fellow-heirs with the saints, through faith in Jesus Christ of Nazareth

(Dan. 7:27, Eph. 2:19). This is what is most important to remember, that God desires a personal relationship with each and every one of us; regardless of our family background, the sins we have committed, what "evils" we have experienced, our financial status, etc.. He says, "Ho, every one that thirsteth, come ye to the waters, and he that hath no money; come ye, buy, and eat; yea, come, buy wine and milk without money and without price." (Isa. 55:1, Matt. 11:28-30). He is the great provider of the free gift of eternal life in Christ Jesus of Nazareth (Rom. 6:23, 2 Cor. 9:15, Eph. 2:8)!

Regarding the saints reigning with Christ for 1000 years; is it not possible that this was part of the selection process, because if one could believe that they could live for 1000 years, is it not also possible to believe that you could have a chance to be like Adam and Eve someday (Gen. 5:5, Rev. 20:4, 6)? The point is, that maybe it was a test of God, in whether or not we actually believe the true account of the Bible, and the possibilities of good things to come (Rev. 21:7)! I will speak about the subject of eternity in another book. Also, if the saints are "sons" or children of God, is it not possible that they will experience time like God does (2 Pet. 3:8)? It is possible that the millennial reign, for Christ and His saints, are like a twinkling of an eye, like a day gone by (Ps. 90:4, 1 Cor. 15:52). Nevertheless, this all remains to be seen. Regardless of this, Christ's Kingdom is and always has been an eternal Kingdom, so the "physical" government of God in the "Messianic Age" is only a portion of His sovereign rule over all things, in all time, in all places (Ps. 103:19)!

Conclusion

Although all prophecy may not have been completely fulfilled regarding the "Messianic Age" prophecies. Jesus was and is the Messiah, the Shiloh, the Redeemer and Lord, King of Israel and the whole earth (Isa. 9:7, Matt. 1:23). In an article about a Jewish Rabbi, Yitzhak Kaduri, it was said he revealed that Jesus Christ of Nazareth was the Messiah, in a note made available after his death in 2007; Faith Today, July/August 2015, pg. 12, Rabbi's legacy sparks revival among orthodox Jews, www.israeltoday.co.il. This is just some proof, but the point is, Jesus is whom He says He is. The New Testament accounts are accurate and true, Jesus is the Son of God, the Son of Man and the Saviour of the whole world! If this entire world knew this one fact and chose to follow this Man, the Son of God and God wholeheartedly, what kind of world would we live in then? A question that we can all consider; prayer for God's kingdom to come, certainly would not hurt (Matt. 6:10). Nevertheless, all in God's good timing (Eccl. 3:1).

Regarding, the Lamb and saints standing on mount Zion (Rev. 14:1). It is spoken of, in various places, whom or what "…Mount Zion…" is. Psalm 78:68 calls, the tribe of Judah, Mount Zion! And Jesus is of the tribe of Judah, through His earthly mother, Mary (Luke 3:23-38, Rev. 5:5). God is mount Zion! And the Holy Spirit working in, and through the Body of Christ, is Mount Zion! Psalm 125:1 says, "They that trust in the LORD *shall be* as mount Zion, *which* cannot be removed, *but* abideth for ever.". In Isaiah 9:6 it describes the child, Jesus, as being the head of the Church. Jesus Christ of Nazareth is the Head, we are the body (Col. 1:18). This is why we need to allow the Holy Spirit to guide our mind, because the Holy Spirit proceeds from God and is the truth (John 14:16, 17). And last, Hebrews 12:22 speaks of "…mount Sion…", the city of the living God, the heavenly Jerusalem. The point is, that God's kingdom is, first and foremost, spiritual; as He is a Spirit (John 4:24). So would Jesus and His saints not also be apart, first and foremost, of this spiritual kingdom, if the "Messianic Age" is literal?

Zechariah 8:23 speaks of people from all nations grasping the robe of a "…Jew…", because they hear that God is with them. This was indeed fulfilled in Jesus, when those whom were looking for healing, would touch His robe for healing (Mark 5:24). But this may be fulfilled on a greater scale in the future, certainly as was said earlier, the Levites will have some sort of responsibility of judging (Ezek. 44:24). Nevertheless, it says, that Jesus will rule with a rod of Iron (Rev. 19:15). And that rod is described as being Israel, or better put the descendants of the 12 tribes of Israel (Jer. 51:19-23, 10:16). The Hebrew word for rod, in the Old Testament, is also used to describe a tribe; Strong's number 4294. That being said the rod may also be described as the Holy Spirit, God's Word, and written Word, the Holy Bible (Isa. 10:17, 11:1). The point is, that God's rod is very likely His people. He uses us to bring His message and commandments, through the written Word and Holy Spirit, to the world!

If Jesus is with God, and is God; How can earth contain Him (1 Kings 8:27, John 1:1, 14, 10:30, 20:28; Isa. 9:6)? His 2nd coming may very well be a process. In our lives, the gospel being preached to all of the nations, the "Great Tribulation", the "Messianic Age" or thousand years of Christ's rule with His saints, the 2nd Resurrection, the final Judgement on the Last Great day, and then the New Heavens and a New Earth (Matt. 24:14, 21; 2 Pet. 3:10-13, John 7:37, Rev. 20, 21, 22)! The point is, that Jesus is the Word and His Word will be fulfilled, whether we see Him physically walking amongst us as an individual again, or not. Regardless, we can experience Him in ourselves; through reading the Holy Bible, praise, and prayer and in each other, through the same (Matt. 25:34-40). Psalm 89:14 says of God, "Justice and judgment *are* the habitation of thy throne…". And Psalm 22:3 says of God, "But thou *art* holy, *O thou* that inhabitest the praises of Israel.". And Jeremiah 31:33 and 34 talk of a time when there will be no need for a teacher, as God's laws will be written in our hearts. This was fulfilled in the outpouring of God's Holy Spirit at Pentecost, seven weeks after Jesus' resurrection, and ten days after His ascension into heaven; but has likely not yet been completely fulfilled in this world yet, as of the early 21st century A.D., as we still have wars, famines, etc. (Acts 1:1-9, Heb. 10:12-18).

Last, Revelation 5:10 says, out of every nation there will be kings and priests. Is this proof that the saints will be in spirit form? And the nations will be following God? And Hebrews 9:16 and 17 talks about where a testament is, there also must be the "…death of the testator.". And Psalm 116:15 says, "Precious in the sight of the Lord is the death of his saints.". Hebrews 12:18-24 clears up these interpretations of God's presence with His angels, Jesus and His saints; it describes the Spiritual nature of His being! The point is, that the Bible makes it overwhelmingly evident that God is a Spirit, and people are to follow His Holy Spirit. The resurrection of saints, the existence of heavenly angels and Jesus Christ of Nazareth, are comforting to know about, so that we realize we are not alone in our trials, and that we have someone or a "host" of God's Holy Spirit to help us and fight for us in our fleshly trials and "mental" battles. But ultimately, He desires to work through us, and in us; through our fellowship with Him in prayer, reading from His Holy Bible, praise or worship, and thanksgiving. He desires us to experience peace, and that comes through reading the Holy Bible and faith; it comes from God's Holy Spirit, in Jesus Christ of Nazareth, God, the Father's, only begotten Son (Isa. 28:9-13, Matt. 11:28). Alleluia and praise the LORD. Amen and Amen.

Discussion: Of God and Man

"As I would not be a slave, so I would not be a
master. This expresses my idea of democracy."
– Abraham Lincoln, 16th US President

Abraham Lincoln, an early President of the United States of America, and a helper in the abolishing of slavery. His words ring very true today, and are exactly how Jesus feels about us. He said, "Henceforth I call you not servants; for the servant knoweth not what his lord doeth: but I have called you friends…" (John 15:15). Jesus' only desire is that we turn to Him, is that we commune with Him, is that we believe in Him and that ultimately, we accept the incredible gift of eternal life in His Holy name (1 Tim. 2:3, 4). His work was already complete on the cross (John 17:4, 19:30). He does not have to do anything else, His earthly suffering for us, was momentary; but His life is eternal, and so can ours be, through accepting the sacrifice He made for us so many years ago (John 16:20-22, 2 Cor. 4:17). He loves us, and desires us to be like Him! To live forever, to be children of the living God! Whom does not change and who has everything, "…with whom is no variableness, neither shadow of turning." (Mal. 3:6, Eph. 4:6, Jam. 1:17). If we had only God's Holy Spirit in us, and had nothing else, we would and do have everything! God's Holy Spirit is the seed of eternal life, it is the seed of all that we see and cannot see (Gal. 3:29, 1 Pet. 1:23, 1 John 3:9). It is so simple, yet so difficult for some to understand, and yet really, we are not called to fully understand God right from the start, we are just called to accept Him and trust Him; one step at a time, so to speak (Jos. 1:8, Job 23:12, Ps. 119:15, Luke 24:45, 1 Cor. 2:9-12, 1 Pet. 2:2). This is the peace of God that passes all understanding (Phil. 4:7)! Understanding, knowledge and having an answer for every question under the sun is great, but it is the peace of God, His rest, that is infinite, eternal and wonderful; a goal worth working towards (Phil. 3:14)! In Jesus Christ of Nazareth, we have that peace; in God's Holy Spirit we have that peace; in God, the Father, we have peace (Isa. 9:6, Rom. 5:1, 2 Thess. 3:16)!

Discussion Questions

1. How can only 144 000 be chosen? What about all of the other Christ followers throughout history? (Hint: Ephesians 2:19).

   _____

   _____

   _____

2. Does the epistle to the Hebrews give a clue to whom will physically be "ruling" earth during the "Messianic Age"? Read Hebrews 2:5-12 to start.

   _____

   _____

   _____

3. If God can make an animal speak, can He not also guide man in ruling this world? Read Numbers 22:28-30 and find other verses that confirm God's sovereignty over all of His creation.

   _____

   _____

   _____

CHAPTER 5

WORSHIP, THE TEMPLE AND ONE GOD

"For verily I say unto you, Till heaven and earth pass, one jot or one tittle shall in no wise pass from the law, **till all be fulfilled.***"*

— MATTHEW 5:18

Introduction

The Golden rule is supposed to be an all-encompassing rule that spans all religions, cultures, and beliefs. It is said to be "…whatsoever ye would that men should do to you, do ye even so to them …" (Matt. 7:12). A proper foundation for a relationship with our Creator ought to be through the knowledge of and faith in Jesus Christ of Nazareth, the chief cornerstone (Dan. 2:34, Rom. 9:22, Eph. 2:20). But we can all progress with this simple "golden rule" if need be. In this chapter, I will talk about the "deeper" things of what the Bible describes as a physical form of worship and offerings to God; that may indeed take place in the future literally or it may not, as of the early 21st century A.D. (Ezek. 43:10, 11). Nevertheless, we must understand that everything stands or falls on the knowledge that Jesus Christ Immanuel of Nazareth was sent by God, He is the Son of God, He died on the cross once for all, for the forgiveness of our sins, He was buried and He arose three days later, revealing Himself to His disciples, on the first day of the week, and ascending to the Father in heaven forty days later, to sit at the right hand of God, so that all whom believe in Him will not perish, but will receive everlasting life (Matt. 1:23, Mark 1:11, 16:19; John 3:16, 17; 1 Cor. 15:3)! This is the key, no sacrifice or offering is any longer required for our salvation as individuals, we have been given an eternal gift of life in Jesus Christ of Nazareth, that will never perish (Ps. 16:10, Acts 2:27, 31; 13:35)!

Temple Worship - Why a temple and offerings?

To understand this, we need to understand the history of the nation of Israel. And it is a checkered one to say the least. Israel came from a line of righteous men, that can be traced back to Shem, after the flood, and to Adam, through Seth, before the flood (Gen. 5). Nevertheless, Israel became God's chosen people (Ex. 19:5, 6). They moved to Egypt after a famine and then they grew large in number, in their place of sojourn (Ex. 2:20, 12:7, Num. 1:46, 26:51). After, at least, a couple of centuries, they were numerous, and God rose up a leader, Moses, to bring them to their "promised land", the land of Canaan (Ex. 3). During their time in the wilderness, on the way to Canaan, the "Law" was developed (Ex. 18-40, Lev., Num., and Deut.). This is also where the Israelite worship, in a temple, in all likelihood developed, with God being at the centre of it in the "...most holy." place with the "...ark of the testimony...", also known as the "...ark of the covenant..." or "...ark of the LORD..." (Ex. 26:33, Num. 10:33, 1 Sam. 4:6). Albeit, the temple structure in the wilderness was actually a tent (Ex. 26:11).

Now this is all grand, but they built a more wonderful temple in Jerusalem, under the reign of King David's son, King Solomon, first; and had at least one subsequent temple rebuild after that (Ezra). The problem is, that early on in Israel's history, in the "promised land"; the Northern ten tribes turned from God, His commandments and His worship service and God gave them up, to go into captivity (1 Kings 12, 14:15, 16; 2 Kings 17). Although at their defence, it was prophesied to happen due to King Solomon's idolatry, and even much earlier; when Jacob prophesied over his sons, the ancestors of the 12 tribes of Israel, for their descendants and the "greater plans" God has for them (Gen. 48, 49; Deut. 33, 1 Kings 11). At any rate, is it not possible that the "Messianic Age" temple, is meant to not only show the world how to "properly" worship God; but also to restore the "...breach..." that took place in the relationship between God, His people the Jews, the tribe of Judah, and His people of the Northern ten tribes, in the "Messianic Age" temple service (Isa. 30:26, 58:12; Ezek. 45:17, 20)?

This could very well be the case, but we must always remember, that Christ has already redeemed each of us as individuals, through His sacrifice on the cross of "cavalry" (Jer. 3:16, Matt. 3:16, Luke 3:16, 23:33; John 3:16, Heb. 9:11-28). Not just for the tribes of Israel, but for ALL nations, tribes and tongues; where ever we come from (John 3:16, 1 Tim. 2:4, 2 Pet. 3:9, Rev. 5:9, 7:9). Most importantly, we must put our trust in Jesus Christ of Nazareth, for the future of our lives and this world, as a whole. In a later book, I will speak about the history of the tribes, and this earth, in general, in greater detail. Nevertheless, we must remember, that God does have a plan for this world, and all whom dwell in it. He is not slack in keeping His promises (2 Pet. 3:9). This is where patience comes in to play, in ongoing developments of His plan for each and every one of us, and this earth as a whole (Luke 21:19).

Levitical Priesthood

Much can be said about the Levitical priesthood. There are a couple important points however; namely Moses was a Levite, as well as Aaron. Through Aaron, a descendant was born, named Zadok (1 Ch. 6:12). And these descendants of Zadok seem to be chosen amongst the sons of Levi, because they continued to guard the sanctuary of the LORD, when the remainder of Israel went astray (Ezek. 44:15). This is important, because according to Ezekiel's account, the sons of Zadok have been chosen to attend to the LORD in His house during the "Messianic Age", if or when the temple mentioned in the book of Ezekiel, is built (Ezek. 44:15, 16). The remainder of the Levites, because of their rebellion, guard the gates and take up other temple positions, outside serving the LORD in His sanctuary, according to Ezekiel's account (Ezek. 44:10-14). Malachi 2 calls the Levite, the "...messenger of the LORD of hosts." (Mal. 2:4-7). Although God has used many "prophets" and "men or women of God", outside of the Levites, to reach God's people and the world; namely, through Jesus Christ of Nazareth; the Levites have always been "set apart", as God's ministers in His sanctuary, and the "...messenger..." on behalf of God to His people (Deut. 33:8-11, Ezek. 44:11, 28-30, Mal. 2:7, Heb. 7:14). Moses is a perfect example; the first 5 books of the Bible are attributed to God's efforts through Moses in one form or another. Namely by Moses' recording of them, although some have suggested he used previous records to do parts of the book of Genesis; which is likely, as I am sure he had help from scribes with most of the work (Ex. 34:27). Nevertheless, Moses prophesied of the Messiah, Jesus, and the books of the law came through God's revelation to him (Deut. 18:15-22, John 5:46).

Malachi 3 sheds more light on what, likely, needs to take place before the "Messianic Age" temple can be built and the Levites can take up their priestly duties. Namely, the "Great Tribulation", must take place in order to cleanse this world and all whom live in it (Matt. 24:21, Rev. 2:22, 7:14). In the book, "Time, Times and a dividing of Time – What did John really see?", I speak about this time mentioned, in the Bible, as the "Great Tribulation" (Matt. 24:21, Rev. 2:22, 7:14). However, I stated at the beginning of that book, that a temple may need to be built and a sacrifices may start up, before the "Great Tribulation"; according to Daniel and Christ's account of the "...abomination that maketh desolate..." prophecy being fulfilled (Dan. 12:11, Matt. 24:15, Mark 13:14, Luke 16:15). However, reading Malachi 3 and thinking about it further, especially reading what an abomination to the Lord according to the book of Proverbs and other places in the Bible can be; the "...sacrifice being taken away..." mentioned in Daniel and in Matthew, may be something more spiritual than physical (Lev., Deut., Prov. 29:27, Isa. 1:13, Jer. 32:35). Like the "...daily *sacrifice*..." of our work or "way of life" being taken away or something like that (Dan. 12:11). More importantly, the main event Malachi is likely talking about, is the "...day of the LORD's vengeance..." or "...year of recompences...", which can be translated as the year of God's wrath (Isa. 34:8, 61:2, 63:4, 66:15-18; Rev. 16). This subject is also discussed thoroughly in that book; and, of course, the Bible, itself, is the best reference for the topic. Only time will tell the truth of these prophecies, however.

Nevertheless, it is not the purpose of this book, to speak about the "Great Tribulation", but what may take place after it, in the "Messianic Age". But in Malachi 3:3 it says "And he shall sit *as* a refiner and purifier of silver: and he shall purify the sons of Levi, and purge them as gold and silver, that they may offer unto the LORD an offering in righteousness.". I believe that this purification, Malachi is talking about, is directly related to the "Great Tribulation", and more accurately "….the day of the LORD's vengeance…", that is to come upon this entire world during the "Great Tribulation", not just the sons of Levi, as of the early 21st century A.D. (Isa. 34:8). The purpose would be, to purify this world and turn it to God's way; to prove His omnipotence, unquestionable existence and sovereign authority over all of His creation (Matt. 24:21, Rev. 2:22, 7:14)! See the various appendices, especially appendices B and F for more details and interpretations on the "roles" of the Levites, sons of Zadok; and their relationship with the LORD and His presence in this possible future temple, as of the early 21st century A.D.. In the appendices, more is spoken about how the LORD may manifest Himself in the temple, to the sons of Zadok; that is, as He has in time past (Mal. 3:4). Regardless, we are protected by God's wrath through the blood of His only begotten Son, Jesus Christ of Nazareth (Rom. 5:9). Thanks be to God and His only begotten Son, Jesus Christ of Nazareth, with His Holy Spirit! Alleluia and praise the LORD. Amen and Amen.

Last, as mentioned many times so far. We need to consider first and foremost our relationship with our Creator, through Jesus Christ of Nazareth, God, the Father's, only begotten Son, with His Holy Spirit. He is our High Priest forever (Heb. 4:14). And we can go to Him, at any time, in any place, and in any circumstance; placing our trust in Him to intercede on our behalf, when we are in need of comfort, forgiveness, relief and provision (Rom. 8:26-39). The God of the Bible, was wholly manifested, in the life of His only begotten Son, Jesus Christ of Nazareth (Col. 1:18, 2:9). He is our advocate on our behalf, and He will always love us, and He will be with us, and in us, even to the end of the "…world." (Matt. 28:20, 1 Cor. 1:8). The entire being of God, can and does dwell, in each and every one of us, as we allow Him to do so (John 14:20, 1 Cor. 3:16, Col. 1:27, Eph. 4:6). This is that phrase, that suggests we are "…gods…", we are the children of God, sons and daughters of the living God (Ps. 82:6, John 5:18, 10:34, Gal. 3:26). God has put eternity or the "world", in our hearts (Eccl. 3:11). Is it any wonder, why we thrive to "live forever", we try everything in our power to stave off death, appear youthful, and chase after the fleeting "cure" for everything that weakens us (Prov. 27:20, Eccl. 1:8)? Adam and Eve, before the fall, were created in the image, after the likeness of God; this is what we were created to be, as well (Gen. 1:26)! Through the fall we succumbed to death, but in Jesus Christ of Nazareth, we have life everlasting. Alleluia and praise the LORD. Amen and Amen.

Princes

There are princes, plural, mentioned in various places in the Old Testament, regarding this "Messianic Age", as well as "…kings…" (Isa. 60:3, Ezek. 45:8, 9). But there is one specific "…prince…", singular, mentioned in the Ezekiel prophecies of the "Messianic Age" temple worship (Ezek. 44:3). Where this "prince" comes from has been speculated. Is it the resurrected King David, is it Jesus, etc.? But I think a more practical approach may be taken. Consider the possibility that a monarchy or various monarchies, existing in the world today, are going to become the princes or "…prince…" mentioned in Ezekiel 40-48. Also, the throne of David has been established forever through Jesus Christ of Nazareth (Mark 11:10). He was recognized as the "…KING…" on the cross (Matt. 27:37, Luke 1:32-33). And Zechariah 12:8 says, "In that day shall the LORD defend the inhabitants of Jerusalem; and he that is feeble among them at that day shall be as David; and the house of David *shall be* as God, as the angel of the LORD before them.". This is likely prophecy regarding the "Great Tribulation", as well. But I believe that God is also trying to say something here, about His plan for re-establishing His authority or at least reaffirming it, through the earthly lineage of the "…house of David…" or possibly from another tribe of Israel (Gen. 49:10, Ps. 108:8, Jer. 31:9, Zech. 12:8, Rom. 4:16, 1 Cor. 12:12). Not to mention, that Jesus was, and is, from the house of David and is, "…as God, as the angel of LORD…"; He is our God (Zech. 12:8, John 1:1, 14, 5:18, 8:58, 10:30-33, 20:8)!

Nevertheless, time will tell the truth of these prophecies. But again we can rest assured, David's throne has been established forever, through Jesus Christ of Nazareth, here on earth, and in the heavens above (Isa. 9:6, 7; Luke 1:32, Acts 2:25-36). Outside of Christ's finished work, there is reference to the fact that David's throne would never be removed, which is likely prophecy of Jesus Christ of Nazareth, as well (2 Sam. 7:16, 17). There has been many books written about the royal monarchy's, throughout the ages, and how some claim that their roots can be traced back to the royal line of David and the Tribe of Judah, in general, e.g. "Symbols of our Celto-Saxon heritage" by W.H. Bennet. The point is, that realistically, these princes could be related to royal lines and monarchies that already exist here on earth today. Would this not make common sense? Monarchies know how to be "princely" and are already used to the "routine" and "formality" of day to day life, in their respective "dominions". Whatever the truth of this matter, God will establish it in His time. If you are interested, see appendix B – Temple People, for more details on this topic of the "…prince…" (Ezek. 44:3).

The law of God

The ordinances of the temple are written out in the latter chapters of Ezekiel (Ezek. 40-46). There is also the law and ordinances of the Old Testament, which have been used by much of Western society, if not the entire world, to form some sort of "justice" system, here on earth. That being said, the Bible says, in many places, that we have turned from God and have not followed His way (Eccl. 7:20, Isa. 53:6, Rom. 3:10-12). So we should not believe, ignorantly, that this world, in its current state in the early 21st century A.D., is earnestly following God, just because the law exists in its written form. That being said, Jesus came, not to abolish the law, but to fulfil it (Matt. 5:17). He set what I believe to be a "higher standard", the standard of love. Jesus knew that we could not fulfil the commands of the law, that is where grace comes in (Matt. 5:27, 28). He said that all the law can be summed up in that, "Therefore all things whatsoever ye would that men should do to you, do ye even so to them: for this is the law and the prophets." (Matt. 7:12).

Regarding this possible future temple and its ordinances, namely, the "offerings"; we need to consider seriously, the purpose and implications, if they are indeed to be literal, and in the future, so as to not undo or get confused about what Jesus did for us "…once for all." (Heb. 9:7-12, 10:1, 10). I believe, that if there is any reason to start up offerings again, it would be to "atone" for "national" sin, rather than individual sin. The Israelites rebelled against God's commandments, even before Christ came in the flesh (1 Kings 12, 2 Kings 17). Old Testament prophecies talk of a time, when the Northern tribes and Judah will be joined again (Isa. 11:11-16, 58:9-12, 61, 62, etc.). Nehemiah 10:33 confirms, that "… sin offerings [are] to make an atonement for Israel…", likely speaking of the 12 tribes, the entire "…house…" of Israel (Matt. 10:6). Jesus Christ of Nazareth died on the cross at Passover, for each of us, for the forgiveness of our sins, shedding His Holy and righteous blood on the cross. He was buried and He arose the third day to give us the hope and promise of eternal life in His Holy name. But the "…breach…" still seems to remain physically, between the tribe of Judah and the Northern tribes of Israel, as of the early 21st century A.D. (Isa. 11:10, 30:26; Rom. 15:12). I think this is the main purpose of the "Messianic Age" temple; physically to restore the "…breach…", and so that the entire house of Israel and the world, for that matter, will be able to worship God in unity in God's chosen city, Jerusalem, in the prophesied "Messianic Age" (Isa. 30:26, Rev. 20:4, 6).

The New Testament speaks much about the temple and indeed much of Jesus' earthly ministry was around it (Matt. 21:12, 13; Luke 2:41-52, 20:1). Jesus had a zeal for God's house and so did His disciples (John 2:13-17, Luke 24:50-53, Acts 2:46, 3:1, 5:20, 21, 25, and 42). He also said, that "…salvation is of the Jews.", but we are now in a time where we worship God in spirit and in truth, because God is a Spirit (John 4:21-24). This is why Jesus came, not to abolish the law, but to fulfil it, and prove that God is indeed above all; that we are to obey and follow Him, not the commands and ordinances of men (1 Cor. 7:23, 1 Pet. 2:16, Gal. 1:10, Eph. 6:6). That being said, Psalm 1:1 and 2 says, "Blessed… is the one whose delight is in the law of the LORD… ". The law of God is perfect and good, it is man who perverts the law and uses knowledge, information and justice, for selfish gain (Ps. 18:3, 19:7, Rom. 7:12). As we all have, broken the law of God (Rom. 3:23). But it is the grace of God, in Jesus Christ of Nazareth, and His sacrificial blood, that redeem us from our sins. We cannot obtain salvation through the "works" of the law, it is through grace we have been saved, by faith in Jesus Christ of Nazareth and this is a gift (Rom. 3:20, 21; Phil. 3:9, Eph. 2:8, 9). Keep this in mind when considering the law of God, and its purposes here on earth.

Much more could be said, but the epistle to the Hebrews speaks of the law of God, and the apostle, Paul, speaks of it in various epistles as he was a member of the Jewish "…Pharisee…" community, before he began his conversion to follow Jesus Christ of Nazareth (Acts 23:6). If indeed we will be celebrating Leviticus 23 Holy days, annually, and the 7th day Sabbath of rest, weekly, in the "Messianic Age"; this should not be seen as a burden, but as a blessing. God gives us rest! This is what His holydays are all about; repentance, true worship, feasting and rest! What more could we ask for in the Almighty God?! In particular, Zechariah speaks of God commanding families from all of the nations, to celebrate the feast of tabernacles; and likely a delegate family from each nation, will go to Jerusalem, during the "Messianic Age", to worship God during that fall feast week (Zech. 14:16-19). There are various organizations in the early 21st century A.D., that currently facilitate groups from around the world, to visit Jerusalem and worship God during the feast of tabernacles; this is likely from the "...shadow of things to come..." (Col. 2:17, Heb. 10:1). And Ezekiel 45 speaks of these Holy days in detail, as well; and would suggest that the annual Holy days will be kept in accordance with the Scriptures (Ezek. 45:13-25).

Now, the Temple offerings, ought to be considered just that, offerings. Like we offer our services and "tithes" in our community and in church, as of the early 21st century A.D.; these offerings at the temple ought to be considered the same. The word, "...sacrifice...", is only used 3 times in Ezekiel's description of the ordinances of the temple; and twice, it is likely, in reference to the "...burnt offering..." of the people (Ezek. 40:42, 44:11, 46:24). The fact of the matter is, when we are giving up an animal to die, so that it can feed us, we are making a sacrifice. The animal loses its life, and the "owner" is losing the opportunity for that animal to produce offspring, or other products; like milk, cheese, butter, etc.. The point is, when we sacrifice anything, even when we eat a tomato, we are making a sacrifice, because the seeds, if we eat, cook or otherwise process them, can no longer be used to produce more tomatoes. And in no place does Ezekiel mention these offerings or sacrifices, as being the atonement for our sins. That is why Jesus Christ of Nazareth still stands as our sacrificial Lamb, as an atonement for ours sins, forever, once for all; sin and trespass offerings or not (Rom. 6:10, Heb. 7:27, 9:7-12; 1 Pet. 3:18)!

Regardless of the law of God or ordinances, etc.; it cannot be stressed enough, that God is not looking for people to follow the "letter" of the law, to fulfill our relationship with Him. He is looking for a person that desires to know Him in the Spirit, first and foremost (Hos. 6:6, Rom. 14:17). He desires to fellowship with us and in us. It is through His Holy Spirit, that the truth of the letter of the law, is revealed anyhow; so why would we not first accept His Holy Spirit, in order to understand how to follow the laws, He created (Dan. 2:22, 1 Cor. 2:10, Eph. 4:6)!? This is the gift God gave to us in the Comforter, the Holy Spirit, in Jesus Christ of Nazareth's Holy name, whom will never leave us (John 14:16). God desires a personal and intimate relationship with us daily, not based on a set of rules; but on a true, open and pure relationship with Him through prayer, thanksgiving, study and fellowship (Gal. 5:18). If the "Messianic Age" temple is to be built, it should not be seen as a burden, neither the "...ordinances..." of it (Ezek. 43:11). People will be called to provide for it, and some will be called to "attend" to it; Princes, Levites, descendants of Israel, the nations of the world, etc.; and they will enjoy going to it to worship, feast and fellowship, God willing (Mal. 3:4). It will be seen and be experienced, in all likelihood, as a spiritual experience; like going to church and worshipping or fellowshipping within community. But we must never forget the fact, that God's Holy Spirit is with us, wherever we go here on earth; He is with us in whatever we are doing, and He is with us with whomever we are with. God's wisdom keeps us, His Holy Spirit gives us life and Jesus Christ of Nazareth, God, the Father's, only begotten Son, is our life (Jos. 1:9, Deut. 31:6-8, Isa. 41:10, Eccl. 7:12, John 6:63, Col. 3:4). Alleluia and praise the LORD. Amen and Amen

Conclusion

It could be argued that there is no need for a temple or offerings any longer, and a lot of New Testament scripture would substantiate that argument. But Ezekiel was told to write all of the laws, ordinances, fashions, form and comings and goings of the temple mentioned in Ezekiel 40-46, "…that they [Israel] may keep the whole form thereof, and all the ordinances thereof, and **DO** them." (Ezek. 43:11). As I had suggested earlier, Jesus Christ of Nazareth has saved us, no other blood sacrifice but His was, is or ever will be sufficient for our eternal salvation. But this temple ought to be looked at in a different way than just for offerings for sins and trespasses; there are 30 outer court chambers, likely for the people to eat their offerings in; inner court singers' chambers and places to "…boil…" and "…bake…" the food in the corners of the outer court, and in the priests chambers (Deut. 14:23, Ezek. 40:17, 44; 46:20-24). See appendix G for an artist's depiction of the "Messianic Age" temple. Is this not the description of a restaurant in some form or another? Maybe this is the way the "Messianic Age" temple should be viewed as, a very "Holy" restaurant. Now this may seem contentious or undermining the significance of the "Messianic Age" temple, but the argument stands; it is a place for community, joy, peace, feasting, and ultimately, praise and worship (Ezek. 44:11)! What more could we ask for in God's house?

Of course, it could also be argued that it is a rather simple "restaurant", when everything is prepared including the "animal" in relatively close proximity; but a farm with a farm house and barn, or backwoods hunting are not much different in regards to the proximity of the "processing" of food. As of the early 21st century A.D., some of us are so removed from where and how we get our food, that it is repulsive for some to even think about taking an animal's life, to eat it. But God gave us all manner of food to eat (Gen. 9:3). Some are more sensitive to the subject than others, and we are not to judge or cause the subject of food, to be a stumbling block, for those whom do not necessarily agree with the eating of meat (Rom. 14:1-23, 1 Cor. 8:13). But that does not change the fact, that people do indeed eat meat today, and likely always will. Nevertheless, as it says in Hebrews 10:1, "For the law having a shadow of good things to come, *and* not the very image of the things, can never with those sacrifices which they offered year by year continually make the comers thereunto perfect.". We need to place our trust in Jesus Christ of Nazareth, for the truth of all this, for our salvation and for our daily life. Even Jesus said, "… Till heaven and earth pass, one jot or one tittle shall in no wise pass from the law, **till all be fulfilled**." (Matt. 5:18). So only in God's time, will the truth be told, of the possibility of a future temple or the "Messianic Age", in general, as of the early 21st century A.D.!

God created us so that He can dwell with, in and through us (Ps. 100:3, 1 Cor. 8:6). All of the physical things that we see and do are either a reflection of obedience to God, or not. He desires a personal relationship with each and every one of us (Jer. 29:11, Heb. 10:19). It has been that way since the beginning, and always will be that way. Why else would He have created us, if not to spend time with Him and fellowship with and help others to follow Him (Mark 16:15, Heb. 13:16, Phil. 1:7)!? Put your trust in Jesus Christ of Nazareth, and He will be your Saviour, and He will be your friend, and He will lead you to where you need to be, whom you need to be with and what you need to do, in this life and in the world to come (Matt. 28:20, 2 Cor. 2:14). For the Levites and the prince, this temple could be viewed as a "job" at a restaurant, where the prince is the "manager" and the Levites are the "servers" and "cooks". Of course, again, this is a simplified description; because they are servants of God and doing more than "managing" and "serving" and "cooking" at a restaurant, but the argument still stands (Deut. 10:17, 18; Acts 10:34, Col. 2:23, Rom. 2:11).

The Word of God speaks to each of us as individuals. We are all members of one body, which is of Christ (1 Cor. 12:27). But each command, although in the letter, says the same thing to everybody, in the Spirit, may need to be applied individually, to each of our own life circumstances, relationships and goals; depending on where each of us are at, on our journey with God, and mankind. This is where the person of God becomes intimate with each of us, as individuals. He knows us like nobody else. He sees us as "…naked…" before Him (Gen. 3:7, Heb. 4:13). There is nothing about us He does not know, and does not desire to know. If we are to become like Him, we need to be open and honest with Him about everything (Prov. 3:6)!

Last, there are many verses that speak of everyone knowing the LORD, His Spirit encompassing the earth, no one needing a teacher, etc., in the "Messianic Age" (Isa. 2:3, 54:13, Mic. 4:2, Joel 2:28, Acts 2:17, Heb. 8:10, 11; 1 John 2:27). Is this not proof, that we are not completely at this point in history yet, at least as of the date of writing this book? We still have many teachers, preachers, lawyers and judges, etc., and more obviously, contentions amongst religions, cultures and nations. Nevertheless, we can experience this type of "Messianic Age" atmosphere, today, with Jesus, God, the Father, and His Holy Spirit, guiding us in our daily life (Deut. 4:36, Ps. 25:12; 32:8, Jer. 31:34, John 6:45, 1 Cor. 2:13). Regarding the "…prince…", if indeed a monarchy is to be related to the princes of Ezekiel's vision; than this is another clear indicator that New Testament belief of the testimony of Jesus Christ of Nazareth, would remain (Ezek. 44:3). Even into a literal millennial rule of Christ with His saints; as most monarchies at least in the West, are as far as I know, associated with the faith of Christ, in one form or another (Rev. 20:4, 6). The epistle to the Hebrews, is a good New Testament book to reconcile for the Levites and all believers alike; because it talks about the Old Testament references, and references the relationship of the Levites and their purpose. But also speaks of Jesus and His ultimate purpose in His relationship with God and us! His atoning sacrifice for our sins! He is the New Covenant, God has made with us. We must never forget this truth! We can have eternal life through faith in and obedience to Jesus Christ of Nazareth, the only begotten Son of God, through His Holy Spirit with us and in us, forever (Heb. 8)!

Discussion: Jesus' Sacrifice

"Happiness and moral duty are inseparably connected."
– George Washington

This chapter was filled with ideas about law, service, offerings, atonement for sin, etc.. Although some may be more interested in the information of this chapter than others, and may desire to learn more about these concepts outside of the writing of this book; it is important to remember that Jesus Christ of Nazareth died on the cross for the forgiveness of the sins, shedding His Holy and righteous blood for us. He was buried and He arose the third day, to give us all the opportunity to receive eternal life in His Holy name, like He has received from God, the Father (John 11:25, 26; Rom. 5:8, 8:11)! This was God's ultimate goal from the beginning, to create mankind in His image, after His likeness (Gen. 1:27, Eph. 4:24, Col. 3:10). God is eternal and He desires us to be as well (John 17:3, 1 Tim. 1:17, 1 John 2:17). This requires that we follow Jesus Christ of Nazareth, accept His atonement for the forgiveness of our sins, and obey Him to the end of our natural life, here on earth, and forever more in the world to come (John 13:34, 15:12; Heb. 10). Because ultimately, this life is not the end of the journey, it is just the beginning. What Jesus desires, is a repentant heart (Ps. 51:17, Matt. 4:17, 9:13). If you are reading this chapter and are questioning whether you are worthy of such a sacrifice the answer is no, but do not worry, Jesus died for us while we were yet sinners (Rom. 5:8, 2 Tim. 1:9, 10, 1 John 4:10). God loves you as a sinner, He desires us to change and become like Him, but He loves you as you are today (John 3:16). The Bible says, "That if thou shalt confess with thy mouth the Lord Jesus, and shalt believe in thine heart that God hath raised him from the dead, thou shalt be saved." (Rom. 10:9). Even this is a gift from God, the faith required to believe is given by God, all you need to do is accept it (Eph. 2:8)! How simple is salvation in Jesus Christ of Nazareth.

Discussion Questions

1. What about the law, was it not "done away with" when Christ came? Look up some New Testament scriptures that verify your argument.

   _____

   _____

   _____

2. What about the princely line? Is David going to be resurrected to become leader of the 12 tribes of Israel in the "Messianic Age"? Or is a descendant of His family or possibly from

another tribe going to be this prince? What do you think? Find some Scriptures to help you with your understanding.

_____

_____

_____

3. This chapter touched on sacrifices and offerings. Although these may be literal or they may not be, in the "Messianic Age". What is God really looking for, in us, and from us, besides offering Him physical sacrifices and offerings? (Hint: Review Psalm 51:17 and Matthew 9:13 for insight).

_____

_____

_____

CHAPTER 6

THE BLESSINGS AND PROMISES

"Then shall thy light break forth as the morning, and thine health shall spring forth speedily: and thy righteousness shall go before thee; the glory of the LORD shall be thy rearward."

— ISAIAH 58:8

Introduction

As was mentioned, at the beginning of this study; it is important to consider a relationship, with our Creator, first and foremost. It may sound exhausting, but everything stands or falls on whether or not we listen to, believe in and follow, what God asks of us (Deut. 30:19). Blessings and abundance are a great thought, and certainly something to look forward to; but as the Bible says, "The LORD *is* good to all…" (Ps. 145:9). So God's goodness is going to come to all, no matter the circumstance. What is more important than, is not the temporary things, because we will inevitably receive them anyhow; but the eternal things, the spiritual gifts (John 3:6, 1 Cor. 6:17). This is where spending time with God; in prayer, praise, reading His Word, the Holy Bible, and fellowshipping with others, comes in (Matt. 6:6, Rom. 10:17, 1 Pet. 2:2, 2 Tim. 3:16). We need His Holy Spirit to keep us alive; so is it not in our best interest to spend time with Him (Jam. 2:26)?

What does the remnant have to look forward to?

It is interesting to consider, that this world could flourish and become like the "…garden of Eden…"; but that is what the Bible talks about (Gen. 2:15). This has happened throughout the centuries and continues. There are deserts, that have become oases', and countries have reclaimed "…waste places…" (Isa. 5:17, 51:3, 52:9, 58:12). A perfect example is Las Vegas; this is a booming town in the middle of a desert, but there are many more places like it around the world; including in Israel proper, some African nations, Dubai and the list can go on, as of the early 21st century A.D.. The point is, that if the "Messianic Age" also has a future fulfillment, as of the early 21st century A.D.; we have much to do about, rebuilding these "…waste places…", dwelling in them and enjoying God in them (Isa. 5:17, 51:3, 52:9, 58:12). This requires obedience to God, vision of course, and some sweat from our brow; but the end result is blessing, after blessing (Gen. 3:19, 15:1; Deut. 11:7). A cup overflowing (Ps. 23:5, Mal. 3:10, John 6:35)!

One of the promises God makes, is that every man will lay under his own vine (Micah 4:4). This may be referring to Jesus Christ of Nazareth; as the TRUE vine, but may also refers to the housing "crisis", that exists, as of the early 21st century A.D., here on earth, being a thing of the past (John 15:1). Another great promise, is universal education; namely, in God's Holy name. Isaiah 11:9 says, "They shall not hurt nor destroy in all my holy mountain: for the earth shall be full of the knowledge of the LORD, as the waters cover the sea.". And Zechariah 14 talks about where this knowledge comes from, in an earthy sense; it talks about rivers of living water coming from Jerusalem; as I had mentioned earlier, there is likely a dual message in Zechariah 14:8, regarding a real stream of water, and the "spiritual" living waters of God's Holy Spirit, flowing out of a "Messianic Age" temple, in Jerusalem (Prov. 18:4, Isa. 2:2, 33:20-24, 59:19-21, Jer. 17:13, Ezek. 11:23, 40-46, John 4:10). The point is, that the God of Israel, Isaac and Abraham; will be the God teaching this world, in the "Messianic Age". This passage, if interpreted correctly, is a perfect example of the duality of the Bible and message of God, which can be both spiritual and literal in nature!

Peace, Love and Happiness

Ezekiel 47 speaks of this river flowing out of the house of God, and describes the waters, as they grow deeper and wider, until they reach the sea, likely the Dead Sea; to heal the high concentration of salt water there (Ezek. 47:8). It describes the river filled with the life of fish, and that everything that comes to it, will be healed (Ezek. 47:9). It also describes trees with fruit, for "…meat…", that is food; and the leaf for "…medicine." (Ezek. 47:12). There is also a river and trees, like these, described in the Book of Revelation; and, of course, in the garden of Eden, in the book of Genesis, in the beginning (Gen. 2:8-10, Rev. 22:1, 2). And there certainly is a relationship, but if it is literally going to take place in the future, as of the early 21st century A.D., this will certainly be one of those signs of God, that would put a person in a position of certainty, about God's abilities, Majesty, Sovereignty and ultimately prophetic truthfulness. I have no doubt that God is capable of bringing a prophecy like this, to come to pass. It is just a matter of time, and waiting for God's Word to be shown true…and it will be!

The tree of life, in particular, is also an interesting topic (Gen. 2:9, Ezek. 47:12, and Rev. 22:2). This is representative of our life; as in the Bible, it also describes us, human beings, as being trees (Num. 24:5, 6; Isa. 61:3, Jer. 17:8). The Bible also describes wisdom, and the fruit of the righteous, being a tree of life (Prov. 3:18, 11:30). The point is, that God has created us, to follow Him, and obey Him. He sees us like the tree of life, if we follow Him; no doubt, Jesus Christ of Nazareth is the ultimate tree of life, here on earth and forever more, indeed! We can bring fruit from the tree of life to our children, and our children's children; this is where teaching "…whatsoever ye would that men should do to you, do ye even so to them…", comes into play (Matt. 7:12). This brings us to Ezekiel 36, 37 and 48; that describes the revitalization and restoration of the lands, and the Holy Spirit to God's chosen people, Israel! Throughout the past millennia, they have been dispersed among the "heathen", starting "officially", about 700 B.C, approximately 700 to 800 years after leaving Egypt for the "promised land"; as mentioned earlier, this land restoration has already been taking place, but has a greater fulfillment, likely, in the "Messianic Age" (Jer. 33, Ezek. 37, 48). Revelation 21 is also an interesting description of the TRUE "final" destination; that is marriage, two becoming one, like Adam and Eve; it describes the "wedding supper" with Jesus Christ of Nazareth and His Church in the New Heavens and a New Earth (Rev. 21:2). It describes the "…new Jerusalem, coming down from God out of heaven…", which should ultimately be everyones goal, here on earth (Rev. 21:2)!

Last, 1 Timothy 6:5 says some may be, "…supposing that gain is godliness…". The point is, that we can, including myself, get quickly caught up in the infinite nature and unending possibilities with God, and we may lose focus on the "main thing". If we are following God, just for means of earthly gain; this is a vain and evil reason for desiring to have a relationship with our Maker. There was a man in the New Testament that thought in a similar way, and desired to pay a sum of money to receive the Holy Spirit; he was rebuked, needless to say (Acts 8:9-24). God did not create us for material success alone; He has everything and created everything, He desires an open and humble heart and mind that He can work with and commune with (1 Sam. 16:7, Ps. 51:6, 2 Cor. 3:18, Eph. 3:16). This is what He desires from us; He gives of Himself, His Holy Spirit freely. This is the gift God gave us, while we were yet sinners, He came, in His only begotten Son, Jesus Christ of Nazareth, and died for the forgiveness of our sins on the cross at Passover, shedding His Holy and righteous blood (Rom. 5:8)! He was buried and He arose the third day to give us the hope and promise of eternal life in His Holy name. We were put here, to lift God up, exalt Him as our Creator, not to try and "fit" Him into some dumb idol; like money, houses, cars, etc. (Ps. 29:1, 2, 96:4-9, 115:1). As the Bible says, "…seek ye first the kingdom of God, and his righteousness; and all these things shall be added unto you." (Matt. 6:33, Mark 10:29, 30). God was, and is glorified in Jesus Christ of Nazareth, God, the Father's, only begotten Son, and He can be glorified in us, if we follow Him, allow Him to live in us, and work through us, with His Holy Spirit (John 13:31, 14:13, 17:4; Rom. 16:27, 1 Cor. 10:37)! This is the key, accepting the Holy Spirit, the Glory of God, to live in us and amongst us and through us! Glory be to God! Alleluia and praise the LORD. Amen and Amen.

God's promises to those whom obey

Regarding events leading up to, and at the outset of the proposed "Messianic Age". God makes many promises, one of them being that He keeps us alive and satisfied, during famine (Ps. 33:18, 19, 37:19). A perfect example of this, is Israel's exodus from Egypt; with Moses and the 10 plagues, amongst the other miracles in the wilderness (Ex. 7-12). Israel was protected throughout this process, in the wilderness they were fed, and even their clothes did not wear out (Ex. 16, Deut. 8:25, 29:5; Neh. 9:21)! If a person were to do some historical research; you might find that in time of war and famine, in the past, there have been accounts of the same miraculous results, as there is nothing new under the sun (Eccl. 1:9, Matt. 6:25-35). Parts of the earth can be flourishing and produce abundant harvest, while other parts are facing drought, famine and disease (Gen. 8:22, Matt. 24:7). This is becoming less of a commonality, as we "progress" as a society, but if the "Great Tribulation" has not taken place yet, as of the early 21st century A.D.; than we still have some trials to endure, before the "Messianic Age" comes fully into existence, here on earth.

Isaiah 14 describes Lucifer, now the enemy, adversary, Satan; as being like a man, or actually a man (Ezek. 28, 31). If this is the case, it is very obvious that the "Messianic Age" is possible; if all of the "evil" men were to be removed from the earth, supernaturally or by war, plagues and famine, etc.. In Zechariah 14:17 it says, that the families of the nations of the earth must keep the feast of tabernacles, and come to Jerusalem to worship the LORD, Jesus Christ Immanuel of Nazareth! And Jeremiah 30:17-22 describes the restoration God has had planned for His people and Jerusalem; although it is likely describing Jesus and His Messianic fulfillment, this may also describe the future "Messianic Age", if it is indeed to be fulfilled literally in the 1000 year reign of Christ and His saints, with the building, of a temple mentioned in Ezekiel 40-46. Joel 2:15-32 describes the tremendous blessings in the prophesied "Messianic Age", but also describes what must take place to reach it; which is the great signs and wonders in heaven, the "…locust…" and the "…terrible day of the LORD…". Although part of this prophecy may have been fulfilled as New Testament scripture, in the book of Acts, at Pentecost, with the pouring out of the Holy Spirit upon Jesus' disciples, fifty days after Jesus' resurrection, and ten days after His ascension into heaven; we have not likely seen the "…terrible day of the LORD…", a part of the "Great Tribulation", completed yet, as of the early 21st century A.D. (Matt. 24:21, Acts 1:1-9, 2:17, 19-20; 1 Thess. 5:2, 3).

That "…day…", which is likely actually a year long, is described in the Book of Revelation, in many other places in the Bible, and I have written a book interpreting that time and the time around it in greater detail, called "Time, Times and a dividing of time – What did John really see?" (Zeph. 1:7). 2 Peter 3 also describes a day, as a day is like a 1000 years, as the "…day of the LORD…" or "…year of recompences…" will likely be completed at the end of earth's present history, when the final judgement, the last great day takes place (Isa. 34:8, 61:2, 63:4; Zech. 1:14, John 7:37, Jude 1:6, Rev. 20:11-15). The "Messianic Age" being a time of peace, but also of judgement, in that, God will judge those, during the "Messianic Age", if they do not follow

His commands, through the Holy Bible, the Levites and His Holy Spirit, in Christ Jesus of Nazareth's Holy name (Ezck. 44:24, Zech. 14:7). The point is, that just because a "Messianic Age" may come, with Satan bound for 1000 years; I would not necessarily suggest, that God will allow everyone to be free, to do anything they desire (Rev. 20:2, 7). He will still be "judging" the inhabitants of the earth, on their behaviour towards Him, and with one another, likely similar to today!

Jeremiah 31:12-14 describes the blessings of Zion and those whom dwell in her. Also, Deuteronomy 28:1-5 describes the tremendous blessings of those whom obey God, because He will set them up above the nations of the earth, like Jesus has been established as King of Kings and Lord of Lords. He will bless us wherever we go, and will bless all the work of our hands! Isaiah 60 describes, in detail, the blessings of both a person and the nation of Israel. It describes us as human beings, as the tabernacle of God, and His light being in us; but also likely describes, the blessings of Jerusalem, and the nation of Israel in the "Messianic Age". The point is, that although God desires us to be blessed, and will continue to bless us all, as this is God's nature (Matt. 5:45). There are still trials to be had in this life, especially if we have not entered into this time of world "utopia" of sorts, spoken of in the Bible, and mentioned in this book, as of the early 21st century A.D.. We can experience the kingdom of God in our daily lives, as God is a Spirit; but we cannot expect to be without trials, as Jesus said, "… In the world ye shall have tribulation: but be of good cheer; I have overcome the world." (John 16:33). We need to focus on Jesus Christ Immanuel of Nazareth, as our ultimate teacher, guide and friend; He is our Saviour, and everything else comes from Him, both life and material blessings alike (Rom. 11:36). If we are to ignore the very Creator of our existence; how can we possibly expect to live an enjoyable, healthy and abundant life here on earth, and eternal life in the world to come?

Last, the bigger picture, is that God desires us to enjoy blessings here on earth, but more importantly, that we become His children in an "eternal" nature, born of His Holy Spirit (1 Cor. 15, 1 John 5:4)! He desires to have us live forever (John 3:16). In order to do this, we need to become like Him (1 Cor. 15:50). And the only way to do that, is through Jesus Christ of Nazareth (Acts 4:12). Adam and Eve "fell" and we needed redemption from the "curse" of death we received, from the inheritance of our ancestors, eating from the fruit of the tree of knowledge of good and evil (Gen. 3:22, Rom. 5). The only way to "reverse" this curse, is to be purified and cleansed with the work of Almighty God and the indwelling of His Holy Spirit, through accepting the purification by the sacrificial blood of Jesus Christ of Nazareth, whom died on the cross at Passover, once for all, for the forgiveness of our sins, shedding His Holy and righteous blood. He was buried, and He arose the third day and lives forever, sitting at the right hand of God, until all His enemies have been made His footstool, the last enemy being death, itself (Rom. 6:10, 8:9, 11; Ps. 110:1, Matt. 22:4, 1 Cor. 15:26, Heb. 9:14, 1 John 1:7)! Jesus Christ of Nazareth was the manifestation of God's Holy Spirit, in the flesh (John 1:1-5, 14; 1 Tim. 3:16). And we can also have this Spirit dwelling in us, guiding us and providing for us, every day of our lives, here on earth; all we need to do is ask Him to come into and take over, our life; body, mind and soul (Luke 11:13, 1 Cor. 3:16, 12:3; Rom. 10:9). This is the key to receiving God's promises; it is with obedience to and following God's plan for us! As Jesus said, to pray to God, "Thy kingdom come. Thy will be done in earth, as *it is* in heaven." (Matt. 6:9, 10). Are you ready for this type of commitment? Because God is ready for you!

The change in the nature of life

Isaiah 11:6-10 is an incredible description of the "Messianic Age". It says, "The wolf also shall dwell with the lamb, and the leopard shall lie down with the kid; and the calf and the young lion and the fatling together; and a little child shall lead them. And the cow and the bear shall feed; their young ones shall lie down together: and the lion shall eat straw like the ox. And the suckling child shall play on the hole of the asp, and the weaned child shall put his hand on the cockatrice' den. They shall not hurt nor destroy in all my holy mountain: for the earth shall be full of the knowledge of the LORD, as the waters cover the sea. And in that day there shall be a root of Jesse, which shall stand for an ensign of the people; to it shall the Gentiles seek: and his rest shall be glorious." (Isa. 11:6-10). Although this could be describing the "spiritual" nature of life, even in our day to day lives, as of the early 21st century A.D.; think about the circus animals, domesticated livestock, pets, and zoo animals, that man has been able to "tame". Does this not make it more plausible to happen everywhere? If indeed it is literal and has a "Messianic Age" fulfillment, what an amazing experience this would be alone! That being said, Jesus Christ of Nazareth, is that "…root of Jesse…" (John 8:58, Rev. 22:16).

Ezekiel 34 is a very beautiful passage, it describes the transformation that has been taking place, and will continue to take place in this world. Namely, that the "shepherds" of God's flock have failed and that God is going to take over leading His people. This description lines up perfectly with the idea, that God's Holy Spirit, has been and will be poured out in the "Messianic Age". God will lead His people (Ezek. 34)! There are other verses that describe, what has already been taking place here on earth throughout history, and will likely continue to take place, in greater form, during the "Messianic Age"; that is, that the elderly will sit in the streets, and children will be playing in the streets, essentially freedom from fear of thievery, murder, swindlers, and all kinds of other evils, that plague parts of earth today (Zech. 8:4, 5). As well, people will be choosing peace, that is weapons will be beaten into plowshares (Mic. 4:3). Also, people will be healed from all sorts of diseases (Isa. 33:20-24, 35:3-6; Jer. 30:17). We must remember that all of these verses were fulfilled in the life of Jesus Christ of Nazareth, the Messiah; he healed the sick, gave sight to the blind, cast out devils, walked on water, forgave sins, brought manna from heaven and He lives (Matt. 14:13-21, 22-33, Mark 1:34, John 6:32-39, 9, 20, 21)! He was, is and always will be, a perfect example of the Kingdom of God (Matt. 3:2, 10:7; Mark 1:15, Luke 10:9). So we can partake in these miraculous healings today! However, if there is a literal "Messianic Age" in the future; we can continue to put our hope in Jesus Christ of Nazareth and the possibility of a "…garden of Eden…" like atmosphere here on earth, in our daily life today, and in the possibility of a so called "Messianic Age" (Gen 2:15)!

Another wonderful verse is, "And in this mountain [God's government/Mount Zion] shall the LORD of hosts make unto all people a feast of fat things, a feast of wines on the lees, of fat things full of marrow, of wines on the lees well refined. And He will destroy in this mountain the face of the covering cast over all people, and the vail that is spread over all nations." (Isa. 25:6-7). God has already, with Jesus, and will continue, to remove the vail of lies, "religious" deception and spiritual blindness of His people. Many of His people have become blind spiritually, because they turned from Him; first, in the garden of Eden and then again when the Northern 10 tribes of Israel rebelled against God and His ordinances (Gen. 3:22, 1 Kings 12). This is why Jesus came, to restore sight to the blind, literally and spiritually; this was the miracle that arguably no other prophet or "man of God" had ever done in the history of the Bible; with the exception of Elisha praying to God to blind and then asking God to heal the blindness of a foreign army (2 Kings 6:18-20, Ps. 146:8, John 9)! God admonishes in Revelation 3:18, to anoint our eyes with eye salve, to heal us from our spiritual blindness! Also Revelation 21:4 speaks of our former memories, sins, passing away; although this verse likely fulfils itself at the very end of earth's present history, we can still know that God does not desire us to remember bad memories, sins, evils, negative thoughts, etc. (Phil. 4:8).

All of this is wonderful and grand to think about, but we must remember, in order to experience these blessings spiritually or naturally, we must obey our Creator. We cannot expedite these experiences to this world; they will develop in God's good timing (Prov. 19:2, 21:5). As I had said earlier, the order of service is worship and praise God, learn teachings and study and then act or present an "offering". We must focus on the simplicity of obeying God in our daily life, in order to produce the fruit of God's Holy Spirit (John 15:16, Gal. 5:22, 23). One of them being longsuffering or patience; as the Bible says, "In your patience possess ye your souls." (Luke 21:19). God is doing a glorious and wonderful work, here on earth, and has much more planned in eternity (Ps. 40:5, 96:3; Isa. 55:8, 9). We must take each day, as it comes, obey God and leave the rest up to Him (Rom. 3:4). If we attempt to take our Maker's place, then we are only starting the cycle all over again, like in the garden of Eden, thinking we know better than God (Gen. 3:22). We all know how that turned out; so keep in constant communication with, put your trust in and worship the True God; whom gave us eternal salvation through His only begotten Son, Jesus Christ Immanuel of Nazareth, with His Holy Spirit. Because, " ...there is none other name under heaven given among men, whereby we must be saved." (Acts 4:12). Glory be to our God. Alleluia and praise the LORD. Amen and Amen.

Conclusion

It ought to be mentioned, that Jesus and God, the Father, said, "For ye have the poor always with you…" (Deut.15:11, Matt. 26:11). And Matthew 5:3 says, "Blessed *are* the poor in spirit…". The fact of the matter is, that we are human and God is God. He owns and maintains everything on earth and in the heavens. We can and will partake in His creation and His plan for it; but we will never be God, the Almighty Creator. We need to be His children, and worship Him and obey Him (Gen. 1:27, Ex. 19:5, Deut. 12:10-19, Jer. 7:27, Gal. 3:26). This is what makes a relationship work, giving and receiving (Luke 6:31, 1 John 4:7, 18, 19). He does not desire to be a tyrant or dictator, but He desires to be our friend. Like a loving family member or friend, here on earth; God desires a loving, caring, intimate and peaceful relationship with His creation (John 15:15). This does not require money or possessions to purchase (Isa. 55:1, Matt. 6:20, John 7:37, 38). God provides it all to us as a free gift (Isa. 58:18, Rom. 6:23, 2 Cor. 9:15, Eph. 2:8, Jam. 1:17)! The ultimate blessing and gift of God, is eternal life, in the name of His only begotten Son, Jesus Christ Immanuel of Nazareth; through His gift of the forgiveness of our sins on the cross (John 3:16). Jesus Christ of Nazareth died on the cross for the forgiveness of our sins, shedding His Holy and righteous blood for us. He was buried, and He arose the third day, to give us the hope and promise of eternal life in His Holy name. Alleluia and praise the LORD. Amen and Amen.

Discussion: Peace

"Of all our dreams today there is none more important - or so hard to realise - than that of peace in the world. May we never lose our faith in it or our resolve to do everything that can be done to convert it one day into reality."
– Lester B. Pearson

Peace may seem like a far off dream to some. But I know, from experience that a person can experience it; if even only as an individual with our Maker, in Jesus Christ of Nazareth, and coming to a place of contentment with our life circumstances, in general (1 Tim. 6:6, 7). As really, this is the only way we will ever truly experience peace (Ps. 29:11, 34:14, 37:37, 85:8, 119:165; John 14:27, 16:33). Jesus Christ of Nazareth is the author and finisher of our faith; we cannot write our own "book of life" for Him, we have to let Him write our name in His "…book of life…" (Heb. 12:2, Rev. 20:12). This is the key, and will be the key to peace on earth; it will be the submission of mankind, slowly but surely, to the Almighty God and Creator, through Jesus Christ of Nazareth, God, the Father's, only begotten Son, denying ourselves, taking up our cross daily and following Jesus (Luke 2:14, 9:23). We must be alert and watching, because Jesus Christ said, there would arise false prophets and people would say, here He is or there He is, at the end of the "world" or "ages" (Matt. 24:24-27). I know I have listened to many different teachers of the Bible and Bible prophecy; and certainly they have all had some knowledge, as the Bible says "… we know in part, and we prophesy in part.", but the ultimate teacher is Jesus Christ Immanuel of Nazareth and His Holy Spirit, with God, the Father (1 Cor. 13:9, Rev. 19:10). He has a still small voice and He will speak to you! In Joel and the book of Acts, it says that, the Holy Spirit would be poured out on all flesh in the latter days, people would dream dreams, have visions and prophecy (Joel 2:28, Acts 2:17). Rest assured that the "ALL", includes you! God bless, and keep the faith (1 Tim. 6:12, 2 Tim. 4:7).

Discussion Questions

1. Have you ever heard the term "peace and quiet"? Such as, someone is looking for peace and quiet. This comes from God; this is a fruit of the kingdom of God! Find some verses in the Bible, that would suggest this is the truth. (Hint: to get started look at Proverbs 17:1, 28 and Exodus 14:14).

    _____

    _____

    _____

2. How can we receive all of these blessings, if Jesus is not "literally" walking this earth, with us, in a "Messianic Age"? (Hint: think about who was sent to us after Jesus ascended to heaven).

    _____

    _____

    _____

3. Prayer, Praise, learning and action. These are all keys to "reaping the harvest" of God's abundance in our life! He created us, not to sit and do nothing at all, and just "will" all the blessings into our life; but we need to do some sort of "work" or "deed" in order to receive many of these physical blessings (Jam. 2:20, 26). That being said, miracles do still happen, so do not discount the unexplainable blessings you receive either; especially the gift of eternal life, that none of us can earn of our own efforts (Rom. 6:23, Eph. 2:8, 9)! What type of godly actions can you take, to receive the blessings you desire, for yourself and others?

    _____

    _____

    _____

CHAPTER 7

SUMMARIES AND CONCLUSION

"For since the beginning of the world men have not heard, nor perceived by the ear, neither hath the eye seen, O God, beside thee, what he hath prepared for him that waiteth for him."

– ISAIAH 64:4

Introduction

In this chapter, I will talk about the general summaries of what was spoken of in each chapter of this book, and discuss the final conclusion of the authorship of this book. Take time, when you read through this chapter, to reflect on what you have been studying. Think about what you may be able to change, or do differently, in your daily routine or life goals, in general; to better experience the peace of God, that He desires all of us to experience with Him, first and foremost, and then with family, friends and others as God wills it (Phil. 4:7).

Chapter 1 – The Purpose - Summary

"...Thou shalt love the Lord thy God with all thy heart, and with all thy soul, and with all thy strength, and with all thy mind; and thy neighbour as thyself." (Luke 10:27). God sent His only begotten Son, to earth, so that all whom believe in Him will not perish, but will receive eternal life (John 3:16, 1 John 4:9). Jesus Christ of Nazareth was, is and is to come (Rev. 1:8). He is the bright and morning star, our Saviour and our God (Matt. 1:23, Luke 2:11, John 8:58, 20:28; Rev. 22:16). The Bible says, "...if thou shalt confess with thy mouth the Lord Jesus, and shalt believe in thine heart that God hath raised him from the dead, thou shalt be saved." (Rom.

10:9). Peace on earth is a great goal, but what is more important, is that we ourselves are saved. If you are still questioning yourself, whether or not you are in a healthy relationship with your Lord and Saviour, ask Him to come into your life, He is waiting at the door (Rev. 3:20)!

Chapter 2 – The Remnant - Summary

The Bible says, "…he shall rule…with a rod of iron…" (Rev. 19:15). It is important to understand, that God created each of us for a purpose. We are not like animals; we did not evolve from some single celled organism. Unless you consider the Holy Spirit, the foundation of life; and He is, with God, the Father, and His only begotten Son, Jesus Christ of Nazareth. We came from Adam and Eve, and ultimately from God (Gen. 1:27)! Nevertheless, God still has a plan for each of us, here on earth, and forever. Those whom have endured trials throughout earth's present history, usually, come out stronger for it (Rom. 4:20). And He intends His children, the descendants of Israel, and those whom turn to God from all nations, tribes and tongues of the earth, to "rule" with Him (Jer. 10:16, 51:19-23; Rev. 5:9, 10:9). We must also consider the "supernatural" or "spiritual" nature of God and His kingdom; as it is His Holy Spirit, that rules and leads us, ultimately (Isa. 10:17, 11:1-4). Jesus is the ultimate Leader, Ruler and King of all of mankind!

It is possible, that Christ and His saints, will physically rule among the nations; but the power of God and the fulfillment of His Word through the Great Tribulation, the altering of earth's physical appearance and miraculous signs in heaven, may be enough to prove, that He has, is and always will be with us (Matt. 24, Rev. 20:4, 6). It is also, possibly, a test for His saints, to see if they believe, that a man could reign physically with Him for 1000 years; in order to consider the possibility, that a man could live for upwards of 1000 years, namely, like Adam (Gen. 5:5). And that we may all have the opportunity to be like Adam, someday. On top of all of this; His faithful have remembered and worshipped Him for about 2000 years now, as of the early 21st century A.D., in Christ Jesus of Nazareth's Holy name and before that we worshipped Him as the LORD, which He still is (Ps. 18:2, John 10:30). He has revealed Himself to each and every one of us, in His own time (Rom. 1:20). Do we all need to see Him at once? It may be possible, at any time in the spirit, in a dream, in a vision, in each other, at the final judgment, at the wedding supper of the Lamb and/or in the heavenly "…new Jerusalem…", etc. (Rev. 21, 22). As the Bible says of Jesus, "For where two or three are gathered together in my name, there am I in the midst of them." (Matt. 18:20).

Nevertheless, much remains to be seen, but there is one thing for certain, that "…all flesh *is* as grass, and all the glory of man as the flower of grass. The grass withereth, and the flower thereof falleth away: But the word of the Lord endureth forever." (1 Pet. 1:24-25). The point is, that the Bible is sure, God is sure and His Word will be fulfilled, regardless of our own interpretations of it. The truth of the matter is, that Jesus Christ of Nazareth was, is and is to come (Rev. 1:8). He was in the beginning, and is the only begotten Son of God (John 1:1,

3:16). There is no other way to come to the Father, except through Jesus Christ of Nazareth (John 14:6). Trust in Jesus Christ of Nazareth and God, the Father, with His Holy Spirit, and His promises; and He will lead you to your "promised land", here on earth, and into eternity (John 14:2, 3; 2 Cor. 2:14). God bless, and let us all run the race, that is made before us, with endurance, so that on the final day, we can stand before our God and Saviour with the hope, He will say, "…Well done, good and faithful servant; thou hast been faithful over a few things, I will make thee ruler over many things: enter thou into the joy of thy lord." (Matt. 25:23).

Chapter 3 – The 3 R's - Summary

The finished work of the Bible, is as important a point to remember, as the restructuring or building of any physical structure here on earth. There is no doubt in my mind, that the Bible, with its 66 books, has all of the written information required to live here on earth. We need God's Holy Spirit to clarify what is written in the Bible, and to practically apply its teachings to our daily life, but all we need to do is ask God for wisdom and understanding. So when we consider; is Jesus going to literally be walking amongst us, as King of kings, or is it His Spirit working through us, that is going to be guiding us, as individuals and as His body here on earth? This all remains to be seen. But we must trust, first and foremost, that God is above us all, through us all and in us all; in order to be at one with God and others here on earth, to get anything accomplished in God's Holy name (Phil. 4:13).

There will be much co-operation needed in order to "restructure" the earth and its inhabitants' day to day lives. But God has made us, as a resilient and enduring kind. He created us, and He knows what we need to live (Matt. 6:8). Even the Israelites were provided for, miraculously, in the wilderness, while they were sojourning for 40 years (Ex. 16, Deut. 8:4, 29:5; Neh. 9:21). There are many miracles mentioned throughout the Bible regarding provision, protection and creation, in general (Gen. 1:1, John 1:1-5). If God has brought humankind this far, He can, no doubt, bring His people through "Great Tribulation" to rebuild, live for and worship Him unto the end of this earth, in the "Messianic Age", as of the early 21st century A.D.. Alleluia and praise the LORD. Amen and Amen.

Chapter 4 – The Government - Summary

The government will rest on His shoulders (Isa. 9:6). If we are the body of Christ, and the government will rest on His shoulders, is it not possible that Christ will reign on earth during the "Messianic Age", through His chosen people, and represented in another literal prince; from the ancient lineage of King David or from another Israelite tribe, that, undoubtedly, exists here on earth today; as ancient Israel did in time past, and as certain nations currently do today, in the monarchies of this earth (1 Sam. 16:13, Isa. 22:22)!? Another point should be mentioned here, regarding the "Messianic Age"; the Bible does a great job of reassuring true believers, that we will never perish, never die, etc., and that those whom obey God will do His commands forever, will be blessed forever, etc. (2 Kings 17:37, Ps. 111:7, 8; John 6:51, 10:28, 11:26, 1 Pet. 1:4). Even in Ezekiel it says of God, "...I will dwell in the midst of the children of Israel for ever..." (Ezek. 43:7). The point here is, that although this earth's present history may have a finite "end" (Dan. 12:4, Matt. 24:6, 2 Pet. 3, Rev. 20:11). God's kingdom is, first and foremost, a spiritual one (John 4:24). God is a Spirit, so we must keep that in mind, when seeking His kingdom and righteousness, literal "Messianic Age" or not (Matt. 6:33).

Regardless, it can be interpreted, that Jesus will manifest Himself, during the "Messianic Age", in body and reign from Jerusalem, along with His saints; or it could be, that the saints will be in spirit form reigning with Christ, in His heavenly Kingdom from Jerusalem, on earth (2 Pet. 1:13-20). As the Bible says, "...flesh and blood cannot inherit the kingdom of God..." (1 Cor. 15:50). That being said, Jesus can and will manifest Himself, where and when He desires, regardless of whether or not we know that it is Him; that is, through entertaining angels, Jesus after His resurrection being unrecognizable, Jesus' Holy Spirit in the people we help, and in us, etc. (Matt. 25:40, Luke 24:15, 16; Heb. 13:12). Not to mention, that some of the saints were seen resurrected in the city after Jesus' resurrection (Matt. 27:52, 53). Not that these appearances should be confused with the final resurrection or Christ's coming again (2 Tim. 2:18). But the point is, He lives, and we do and will live in Him and Him in us, in His resurrection promise and in God, the Father, Almighty, through the life giving breath of God's Holy Spirit in Christ Jesus of Nazareth's Holy name!

Chapter 5 – The Temple - Summary

Although the Levites were set apart to serve God, amongst the 12 tribes of Israel; through Israel's rebellion, many of the Levites, also lost their former positions, as well. God has reached out to Israel, and this world, in general, through many prophets, men of God, etc.; not entirely from the tribe of Levi, but God's purpose for the Levites, has been, since Moses, to be His voice to the people (Num. 1:49, 40; Mal. 2:4-7). This must be considered, when we think about where the "saints" and Jesus will be, during the "Messianic Age", if it is literal. God uses people and He gave earth to mankind (Ps. 115:16). Not to say that "angels" do not exist, and they cannot appear to people at times; but more importantly, we need to trust in God's Holy Spirit, working in, and through us, as members of His body, to fellowship (Ezek. 11:23, 47:1-12; Zech. 14:4-8, Mal. 4:2, Matt.17:2, John 4:10, 2 Pet. 1:19, Rev. 1:16, 10:1). We have One God, and we are to worship Him; not angels or other people, even Jesus taught that (Matt. 19:17, Mark 10:18, Luke 18:19, 1 Cor. 8:6)!

If Jesus is with God, and is God; How can earth contain Him (1 Kings 8:27, Mark 16:19, Rev. 3:21)? His 2nd coming, may very well be, a process. In our life, the gospel being preached to all of the nations, the great tribulation, the "Messianic Age", the 2nd resurrection and final judgement, and then the new heavens and a new earth, with a new Jerusalem (2 Pet. 3:10-13). The point is, that Jesus is the Word, and His Word will be fulfilled, whether we see Him physically, walking amongst us as an individual again, in this lifetime, or not. Regardless, we can experience Him in us, and in each other, through His Holy Spirit (Matt. 25:34-40). Jeremiah 31:33 and 34 speak of everyone knowing the Lord, through the indwelling of His Holy Spirit, no doubt (1 John 4:13). This is important to understand, because our bodies are temples, as well. Jesus spoke of His body, being the temple of God in John 2:19. It cannot be stressed enough, that we must remember that we are temples of God. God gave us a body, so that He can dwell in and with us (1 Cor. 3:16, 6:19). This is the intimate marriage like relationship, God desires with us; that is reflected in our physical marriage relationship, between a man and woman, as "…they are no more twain, but one flesh." (Gen. 2:24, Mark 10:8, Eph. 5:31, 32). He also desires us to be, one with Him, spiritually!

Chapter 6 – The Blessings - Summary

Some might have difficulty comprehending a sacrificial system being established again, with a temple in Jerusalem. For many reasons, one of them being, because it is suggested that Jesus "did away with sacrifices" (Heb. 10). However, if the Ezekiel's vision of a temple is to be literal and has a "Messianic Age" fulfillment in this world, as of the early 21st century A.D.; think of it similar to the mystery of Immanuel, God with us (Isa. 7:14, Matt. 1:23). Jesus was, and is, the Son of God, but is also God (Isa. 9:6, 7; Matt. 28:18; Luke 2:11, Eph. 2:14-17). He was, is and is to come, the Alpha and the Omega, the beginning and the end (Rev. 1:8, 22:13). Christ has given us life forever, through His body (John 6:51)! But think about today, with restaurants, meat processing facilities and farms. Are we really doing things any different than what this Temple would be doing, only out in the open air? Not really, but it is more about perception in the early 21st century A.D., than anything else, and of course, health standards in various countries for processing food, for mass consumption.

Nevertheless, the blessings from God, come from obedience to God. Not from man's commandments or our own human efforts. We need to submit to God, and His plan for us, as individuals, first and foremost; in our own life, today, in order to receive God's peace, love, rest and abundance in this life. God loves us and He created us to be happy, healthy and to live a long and fulfilling life with Him and others, here on earth. The key is to take life, day by day; not worrying about tomorrow, or all that may take place in the year ahead, or in our life, in general (Matt. 6:34, Jam. 4:13-15). God is in the "present" as I have often heard; He desires us to be in the present, as well (Jos. 1:9, Lev. 26:12, Ps. 16:8, Prov. 15:3, Isa. 43:2, 52:12; Zeph. 3:17, Matt. 1:23, 28:20; Mark 1:15, 1 Cor. 3:16). This is where we come into full communion with Him and others, not worrying about what was or will be, but just enjoying the presence of God and our fellow man. To God be the Glory through Jesus Christ of Nazareth, His only begotten Son, with His Holy Spirit! Amen and amen!

Conclusion

Think about "...the peace of God, which passeth all understanding..." (Phil. 4:7). It may be a challenge, at times, to envision a time where the world is completely peaceful, perfect and living in harmony, with its Creator. But that is, exactly what the Bible says. If there is meant to be a time of peace on earth, such as described in the Scriptures and in this book, but you cannot understand how it may come about, that is ok. That is, the peace of God. We can experience it, in our daily life, if we accept Christ into our life and let Him lead us (Eph. 2:14)!

Regardless of what takes place in this generation, or the future of this world. Jesus made it clear, and simple; "...love the Lord thy God with all thy heart, and with all thy soul, and with all thy mind, and with all thy strength...And...Thou shall love thy neighbour as thyself." (Mark 12:30, 31). Other than that, whatever will be, will be (Matt. 6:34, Jam. 4:13-15). God has made a promise to those whom partake in His covenant relationship with Him, that His Words will not be removed out of our mouth, neither out of the mouths of our descendants, forever (Isa. 59:21). This is kind of like a "life time guarantee", for those whom follow the true God; that they will be marked with His seal throughout all of their generations, here on earth, and forever more (Jer. 31:31-34). Of course, this covenant relationship was sealed through the ministry and promises of Jesus Christ of Nazareth, the only begotten Son of God, the Alpha and the Omega, and the Bright and Morning Star (Rev. 22:13, 16). And this is why it is so important, that we be a "good" example for our families, and this world, in general; so as to not be a stumbling block between them and God, in this generation, the next and those after them, forever more!

Last, although this book describes what the remnant may experience, what they must choose to do, and what life may look like when they make it through to the "other side". My words could not possibly justify the unending blessings, peace, joy, happiness and general wellness of humanity, upon Christ's prophesied return. We will only know how to describe it, when we actually experience it. So with that being said, let us pray, come Lord Jesus, come! And until that day arrives, let us remember that He is indeed with us, here, in spirit and in truth; in our prayers, in fellowship and dwelling in our body, mind and soul, as we accept Him, now and forever more (Deut. 31:8, Jos. 1:9, Isa. 41:10, 43:2; Matt. 28:20, John 14:16-21). To God be the Glory!

Discussion: Life

"...I am come that they may have life, and that they may have *it* more abundantly."
– Jesus Christ of Nazareth, John 10:10

The Bible says, "...at the name of Jesus every knee should bow...And *that* every tongue should confess that Jesus Christ *is* Lord..." (Phil. 2:10, 11). This does not necessarily mean that they will be saved, because Jesus said, not everyone that says, "...Lord, Lord..." will enter into the kingdom of heaven (Matt. 7:21). Even though everyone is God's, and God has created everything, and everyone for His purpose; we must truly and earnestly desire Him, listen to Him and follow Him daily, to receive the abundance of life. The truth is, that this life is only a small amount of time; we can try and "jam" in all kinds of material things, people and experiences, but we must also consider that God is giving us much more than this life here on earth (Rev. 21:7). He is giving us a life, that will not perish (John 11:26). We may "die" someday, but ultimately we will have a resurrected body if we obey God and follow Jesus Christ of Nazareth, with His Holy Spirit, to the end (John 3:16). He will give us the life that does not die; He will give us an incorruptible body, that will last forever (1 Cor. 15:53). Jesus said, "In my Father's house are many mansions: if *it were* not *so,* I would have told you. I go to prepare a place for you. And if I go and prepare a place for you, I will come again, and receive you unto myself; that where I am, *there* ye may be also." (John 14:2, 3). It may not be 100% obvious, where that place is today; but I suspect it will be like the "... garden of Eden...", as the Bible says, "... a new heaven and a new earth..." (Gen. 2:15, Isa. 65:17, Rev. 21:1). The point is, that life in Jesus Christ of Nazareth is abundant, because it will last forever!

Discussion Questions

1. With all of these ideas, "rules" and changes that may be required in order to fulfil the reality of the ideas written about in this book, regarding the "Messianic Age"; how can we live the truth of the lessons of the Bible, based on some of these more detailed "prophecies", without losing sight of the simple message, that the Bible ultimately puts forth?

   _____

   _____

   _____

2. If Jesus was, is and is to come, the Lamb of God, whom sacrificed Himself once for all, for the forgiveness of our sins; how could God ever accept animal offerings again? See Psalm 22:29 to start.

   _____

   _____

   _____

3. In the end, we need to focus on the "main thing"; that is, Jesus died on the cross for the forgiveness of our sins at Passover. He was buried, and He arose three days later, to show us that we also can live forever, if we believe in and follow Him, whole heartedly to the end. What changes or new "practices" can you make in your daily routine, to better reflect, a life lived for Jesus Christ of Nazareth, God's only begotten Son, and God, the Father, through His Holy Spirit, first and foremost?

_____

_____

_____

AFTERWORD

There is a lot of information, in this book, to dwell on. If the "Messianic Age", is to be a literal time, here on earth, as of the early 21st century A.D.; it would not be possible for me to describe exactly what it may look like or how to detail everything that would be required on every level of governing. We all must leave some room for the Holy Spirit to work, in each of our lives, and in this world as a whole, to bring about any reality (Amos 3:7, 8). So that being the case, you can use this book, as a sort of general guide, to what some of the "Messianic Age" infrastructure may look like, and develop into, if indeed that "age" is to be true, here on earth, at some point in time in the future, as of the early 21st century A.D.. As well, there are many other books, authors, preachers, etc., that speak of the "Messianic Age" with the Holy Spirit, Christ and God, the Father, ruling over the earth, sovereign.

It is not, and will never be, my purpose to explain any of God's promises, prophesies and commands in perfect detail; as only God can reveal His truth to each and every one of us (Amos 3:7, Acts 2:16-21). But as some of my other writing has suggested; we must follow God, invite Him to dwell in us, with His Holy Spirit, read His Word, the Holy Bible, and fellowship with other believers, to discover His Holy Spirit in each and every one of us. To this end it is hoped, that this book is used, as a help to any believer or those whom think they are being called by God, to live a more just, loving and righteous life with Him, in Him and Him in you, here on earth, and forever more (John 15:1-5). As the Bible says of God, "Justice and judgement *are* the habitation of thy throne: mercy and truth shall go before thy face."; speaking of God, Jesus Christ of Nazareth, God's only begotten Son, and His Holy Spirit (Ps. 89:14). He dwells in each of us, if we accept Him, through His Holy Spirit (Eph. 4:6). Do you desire God to live in you? Invite Him in…

I have often heard, there is a "sinner's" prayer. That any of us can pray, submitting to God and admitting that we are sinners and that we need forgiveness for our sins, through Jesus Christ of Nazareth, the Holy Spirit conceived, Son of God. Jesus died on the cross for the forgiveness of our sins, shedding His Holy and righteous blood for us at Passover. He was buried, and He arose the third day for our hope and promise, that we can live again, through believing in

Him (John 3:16). And you certainly can pray to God, through Jesus Christ of Nazareth, this prayer, admitting that you are a sinner and asking Him for the forgiveness of all of your sins and asking for Him to come into your life. But the prayer that Jesus gave us will do well for anyone who desires to start a prayer life; it is "...Our Father which art in heaven, Hallowed be thy name. Thy kingdom come. Thy will be done in earth, as *it is* in heaven. Give us this day our daily bread. And forgive us our debts, as we forgive our debtors. And lead us not into temptation, but deliver us from evil: For thine is the kingdom, and the power, and the glory, for ever. Amen." (Matt. 6:9-13).

APPENDICES

APPENDIX A

Jesus Christ and the 144 000 – Literal, Spiritual or both?

This topic could take a book in itself to study; but the purpose of the 144 000 in a nutshell, is to expand God's eternal kingdom (Isa. 9:7). The 144 000, whom are also likely the saints; come from those whom have been chosen throughout history, from at least, according to Revelation 7, the twelve tribes of Israel, excluding Dan, likely because of his idolatry and rebellion (Jud. 17, 18). Nevertheless, it is possible that there may be more than 144 000 saints; how many more is unsure. Some possible saints; like, Enoch, Noah, Abraham and Isaac, were not from the 12 tribes; but the 12 tribes of Israel came from them. Although I am not an expert, on whom becomes a saint, and whom does not; the number 144 000 is surely a good estimate, likely, to say the least.

Why 144000

144 000 divided by 6000 years of man's rule, equals 24; each year of man's rule. Is it possible, that God always had a few chosen followers, continuously existing on earth; praying earnestly, enduring miraculous trials, etc., to both prepare for their reward and help shepherd God's people here on earth throughout history? Possibly. This still does not answer the question of, why the specific number; but with the perspective of a need for a specific number to "shepherd" over large quantities of people, the number is no doubt perfect, because God purposed it! These saints or 144 000, are chosen by God. They are the men and women, whom have been called, tested, overcome trials and God has chosen, to continue to preach His message of His salvation plan, to all the inhabitants of this present earth. They are considered the firstfruits of God, Jesus Christ of Nazareth being the chief cornerstone, High Priest and Head Apostle of the faith (Heb. 3:1, Jam. 1:18)!

Mount Zion, Mount of Olives and Christ's return with His Saints: Spiritual, Literal or both?

The following is a list of Bible verses, that if understood, in their entirety and compared with any other verses required; relate the possible truth of the event of Jesus' return to earth, at least, regarding the "Messianic Age".

- Psalm 74:2 - **Remember thy congregation,** *which* thou hast purchased of old; the rod of thine inheritance, *which* thou hast redeemed; **this mount Zion,** wherein thou hast dwelt.

- Psalm 74:12 - For <u>God *is* my King</u> of old, working salvation in the midst of the earth.

- Psalm 78:68 - But **chose the tribe of Judah, the mount Zion** which he loved.

- Ezekiel 11:23 - And <u>the glory of the LORD</u> went up from the midst of the city, and <u>stood upon the mountain</u> which *is* on the east side of the city.

- Zechariah 12:8 - In that day shall the LORD defend the inhabitants of Jerusalem; and he that is feeble among them at that day shall be as David; and **the house of David *shall be* as God**, **as the angel of the LORD before them.**

- Zechariah 14:3, 4 - Then shall the LORD go forth, and fight against those nations, as when he fought in the day of battle. And <u>his feet shall stand in that day upon the mount of Olives</u>, which *is* before Jerusalem on the east, and the mount of Olives shall cleave in the midst thereof toward the east and toward the west, *and there shall be* a very great valley; and half of the mountain shall remove toward the north, and half of it toward the south.

- Luke 16:31 - And he said unto him, **If they hear not Moses and the prophets, neither will they be persuaded, though one rose from the dead.**

- Acts 9:4, 5 - And he fell to the earth, and **heard a voice saying unto him, Saul, Saul, why persecutest thou me?** And he said, Who art thou, Lord? And the Lord said, **I am Jesus whom thou persecutest:** *it is* hard for thee to kick against the pricks.

- 2 Thessalonians 1:10 – When **he shall come to be glorified in his saints**, and to be admired in all them that believe (because our testimony among you was believed) in that day.

- Hebrews 12:22 - But <u>ye are come unto</u> **mount Sion**, and unto **the city of the living God**, the **heavenly Jerusalem**, and to an innumerable company of angels…

- Revelation 14:1- And I looked, and, lo, <u>a Lamb **stood on the mount Sion**, and with him an hundred forty *and* four thousand,</u> having his Father's name written in their foreheads.

Of course, any one verse could be picked apart, to attempt to explain a certain "theory". Not to mention the fact, that Jesus did indeed stand on the Mount of Olives, during His earthly ministry (Luke 22:39-44). And He was, indeed, from the tribe of Judah, that would make Him apart of Mount Zion, according to Psalm 78:68. But the point is, that we should not necessarily expect 100%, that Jesus is going to literally and physically reveal Himself to all of mankind, as a man again, at this time in earth's present history, at least as some may expect. Of course, it is possible, and He said that we would see Him coming in the clouds, sitting at the right hand of the power of God (Matt. 26:64, Luke 22:69). So at the completion of the "Great Tribulation", He could reveal Himself for a time miraculously, through nature, or He could literally descend and return to earth (John 12:28, 29; Acts 1:11). This all remains to be seen. But just consider the possibility, that God is working through us, and His Holy Spirit is with us, and in us, as we accept Him. And Jesus is with the Father, and dwells amongst us, and in us, through His Holy Spirit, the Holy Spirit of God (2 Cor. 6:16). This is where the unforgiveable sin comes in. If we blaspheme the Holy Ghost, which is the very spirit that gave us and our ancestors life, so long ago, when life was breathed into Adam, and has renewed us through, our faith in Christ (Gen. 2:7, Eph. 2:5-7). Then what else can we do? Where else is our life going to come from, other than God and His Holy Spirit!?

Acts 9:4 and 5 is a perfect example of evidence of Jesus living through us. As He said to Saul, unconverted Paul, "…why persecutest thou me?" (Acts 9:4). Well Jesus was in heaven by this time. So how would Saul be persecuting Him? Saul was persecuting Jesus, because He lives through the congregation of His saints, and His faithful followers, the Church of the living God! The point is, that we need not worry about whether or not Jesus is literally and physically going to come back to earth, with angels or saints. He is here with us. His Holy Spirit dwells amongst us and He will dwell in you if you ask Him to! Ask and you shall receive (Matt. 7:7).

APPENDIX B

Temple sacrifice verses Jesus' Sacrifice

The united tribes of Israel, as a nation, turned from God, first spiritually, in approximately 970 B.C., namely through king Solomon's idolatry; and Jesus came and sacrificed Himself for us approximately 1000 years later, at Passover in 31 A.D., which is approximately 1000 years for the North tribes and South tribes being divided, before Christ came for all of mankind (1 Kings 11:1-14, Matt. 1). The "Messianic Age" Temple amongst other things, could be purposed for a millennial atonement for those "lost years", before Jesus' final sacrifice, whom died on the cross for the forgiveness of our sins, shedding His Holy and righteous blood, once for all (Rom. 6:10, 1 Pet. 3:18). He was buried and He arose the third day, for our hope and promise of eternal life in His Holy name. The "Messianic Age" temple offerings may represent, "national" atonement of sins, not individual atonement; Jesus Christ of Nazareth was given for each and every individual here on earth, that whomsoever believes in Him should not perish, but have everlasting life (John 3:16, Eph. 2:15)! Also, an important note, the kingdom of God is not, eating and drinking (Rom. 14:17). Even David said in a psalm, that God does not require sacrifices of animals, first and foremost. He is looking for a broken spirit and contrite heart; He desires us to build ourselves, and each other, up in the admonition of the Lord (Ps. 51:15-19, Eph. 6:4).

Greater purpose - the Reunification of the Tribes of Israel with each other and their God!

Ezekiel 43:10 and 11 speak of the command for Ezekiel, and I suppose anyone who is called; to show this vision to "...the house of Israel...", regarding a temple, and its "...fashion...", all of its "...ordinances...", and "...forms...". One particular part, that I had found not to be clear, was the "...building..." and/or "...separate place...", west of the main "...house..." or "...temple..." (Ezek. 41:4, 5, 12-15; 42:1, 10, 13). Thinking of it more critically, it may be the place, that is used to divide the offerings. The word "...separate place..." has a root in cutting or separating; Strong's number 1508. So this may literally be the place, where they separate the flesh, after the altar offering is made, in front of the temple. Others have commented on the subject in various commentaries; one suggestion, is that it is a place for refuse, that may be close to the truth, because there may be waste product that comes out of the butchering process. I do not know. After the next paragraph, is a simplified list of some of the other parts of the temple, including the temple "staff" and guests. See appendix G for a scholar's rendition of the "Messianic Age" temple. The "...separate place...", is likely the building at the rear of the temple, at the centre west side wall of the temple grounds (Ezek. 41:13, 14). This all being said, there are locations on the outside and inside porch of the north and south inner court gates, that seem to be used for the cleaning and dividing of the slain offerings (Ezek. 40:35-43). After the offerings are divided up, at the north and south inner court gates, they are then likely brought to the four corner kitchens of the outer court; this may represent the dividing up of

Jesus' garments into four parts, by the soldiers during Jesus' crucifixion (Ezek. 46:21-24, John 19:23). And the "refuse", may be burned at the altar, so the "…separate place…", may just be a building that is empty. One reference looks at the "Messianic Age" temple grounds, as Jesus on the cross; Jesus' head being the main temple building; the altar, and river as the location of His heart, and representing the blood and water that issued from Jesus' side, when the soldier pierced Jesus' side with the spear, after Jesus gave up the Holy Ghost on the cross at Passover in 31 A.D. (Ezek. 43:13-27, 47:1-12; John 19:33, 34). See, http://ezekielstemple.blogspot.com/, retrieved 20/02/2019, for details.

In general, the "Messianic Age" temple, has an outer and inner court, the entire place may be considered "…the sanctuary…", but it also has an, inner sanctuary or holy place, and most holy place, separated by a wall and doors (Ezek. 41:4, 21). The entire complex may be considered "…the temple…", but it also has a "…house…" within it, that may also be considered "…the temple…" or inner temple (Ezek. 41:1, 5). These steps of purification, are an example of God's order, in separating us from our sins, and preparing us for Him (Rev. 21:2). These buildings within buildings, or rooms within rooms; separate the "…holy…" from the "…unclean…", and this is exactly what Jesus did for us (Ex. 3:5, Lev. 5:2, Matt. 25:32, 33). We cannot enter into eternal life, except through Jesus, and nobody comes to the Father except through Jesus Christ of Nazareth (John 14:6, Acts 4:12). The "Messianic Age" temple is a perfect example of the separating God, Jesus Christ of Nazareth, God, the Father's, only begotten Son, and His Holy Spirit, does; in purifying our body, mind and soul, preparing us for eternal life (Matt. 7:13-14). After all, God considers us His temple; as it says in 1 Corinthians 6:19, "What? know ye not that your body is the temple of the Holy Ghost *which is* in you, which ye have of God, and ye are not your own?". When considering the details of the "Messianic Age" temple and its ordinances; consider how this temple compares to our relationship with God and our fellowman. Consider the reality of your own body as God's temple, and how you relate to others; specifically in the covenant relationship between husband and wife (Eph. 5:25-33).

Temple details

- The House, Sanctuary or Temple in the Inner Court
  - The place the sons of Zadok serve the LORD in, where the most holy place is located (Ezek. 41:4).

- The Inner Court
  - The location of the inner temple, "…house…" or inner sanctuary; holy place and "…most holy place…" where the sons of Zadok serve the LORD (Ezek. 40, 41:4, 5; 43:5, 44:17, 27; 45:3). The temple within the inner court, would be comparable to the tabernacle in the wilderness or Solomon's temple in purpose; with an outer chamber, the sanctuary, and inner chamber, the most holy place,

separated by a "…curtain…" or a wall and doors (Ex. 26:31-33, 1 Kings 6:16, 31, 32; Ezek. 44:27, 45:3).

- The Outer Court
  - For the sons of Levi, whom are in charge of the temple grounds, and the people bringing offerings to the LORD. Likely, similar to the court in the Old Testament temples, also similarly mentioned in the book of Revelation (Ex. 27:9, Ezek. 10:5, 44:9-14; Rev. 11:2).

- The People
  - Those whom bring offerings, and, possibly, share in the eating of their offerings, in the chambers of the outer courts, and at the east gate on the Sabbaths and new moons, etc. (Ezek. 44:11, 16; 46:3, 9).

- The Priests - Sons of Zadok
  - Sons of Zadok, Priests that serve the LORD in the "…house…" in the Inner Court (Ezek. 41:5, 44:15-31).

- The Levites
  - The sons of Levi, that are in charge of the temple gates, and may divide the offerings for the outer courts, and minister to the people (Ezek. 44:10-14).

- The Prince
  - The prince gives offerings, and is allowed, at least, to the threshold of the east gate of the inner court (Ezek. 45:17, 22-25; 46:2, 4-8, 10). The relationship between him and the people must be very much similar. As he, in the "…midst…" of them, will "…go in…and …go forth." (Ezek. 46:10). Jesus very much fulfilled this relationship, during His earthly ministry; and if this is to be fulfilled similarly again, in the "Messianic Age"; then this prince will, no doubt, be with the people in a very godly, but natural way (Matt. 18:20, Acts 5:31). God is no respecter of persons, that is (Acts 10:34, Rom. 2:11).
  - As mentioned in chapters four and five, he could actually be a sign of God's sovereign rule in the "Messianic Age", through Jesus Christ of Nazareth's Holy Spirit, whom we can all partake in (Ezek. 44:1-3, Zech. 12:8, John 14:16).
  - Personally, I believe that Zechariah 12 clarifies whom the prince will represent. If indeed the prince comes from a tribe of Israel and may be a representative of the "…house of David…", then he will indeed have the "…Spirit of the LORD…" resting upon his shoulders (Ezek. 11:5, Zech. 12:8). It will be as if he is a "manifestation" of God, on earth. Of course, he will not actually be God, but God's Holy Spirit will be with him, and he will be a sign or signet of God's presence, during the "Messianic Age" (Rev. 20:4, 6). Ezekiel makes clear that he will have children and descendants (Ezek. 46:16-18). And the prince will

likely die, just like every other human being dies naturally; but his family line will maintain the position of "…prince…" (Ps. 18:50, Ezek. 44:3). Just like the monarchs of our world do today!

- o Last, the tribe of Ephraim is mentioned in the Bible to be God's firstborn (Jer. 31:9). And the Bible says that the "…sceptre shall not depart from Judah…until Shiloh come…" (Gen. 49:10). The point is, that Jesus has come as Shiloh, but in the "Messianic Age", the living waters, mentioned in chapters three, four, six, and in this appendix, and the temple; may also be the continuation of the fulfillment of Shiloh (Ezek. 47:1-12, Zech. 14:4-8). The meaning of which, is rest or tranquility. Jesus Christ of Nazareth is the fulfillment of rest, He is love and we can rest in God's love (Ps. 62:1, 2; Matt. 11:28, 1 Pet. 3:4, 5:7; 1 John 3:19). And the "Messianic Age" is a time of rest from all sorts of burdens. The Bible also says that Ephraim is the "…strength…" of God's head; is it possible, that this is the tribe, to take over earthly authority or ruler ship in the "Messianic Age" (Ps. 108:8)? Joseph, Ephraim's father, was certainly a grand example of ruler ship and authority, when the Israelites came into Egypt to sojourn (Gen. 47). Nevertheless, Jesus will always be King of Kings and Lord of Lords, and He, indeed, descended from the tribe of Judah and king David (Ps. 78:67, 68; Matt. 1:1, Luke 1:32, 33; 3:23; Rom. 1:3, 1 Tim. 6:15, Rev. 19:16). Even Jesus' earthly father's paternal lineage from David is mentioned in Matthew 1, although Jesus was conceived by the Holy Spirit, in the virgin, Mary, espoused to Joseph, both of whom were from the tribe of Judah (Matt. 1:18, Luke 3:23-38). The point is, regardless of which tribe this "princely" line comes from, Jesus is King over all!

- The LORD

  - o The Glory of the LORD enters the temple through the east gate, and it is to be shut behind Him (Ezek. 44:2). In the temple, itself, it says of God, that it is "…the place of…[His]…throne, and the place of the soles of…[His]…feet…" (Ezek. 43:7). This could be literal and God's Holy Spirit may enter through the east gate, and He could physically manifest Himself, in the temple or this may be representative of His presence (1 Sam. 4:4, Ps. 80:1, 1 Chr. 28:2, 2 Chr. 6:1, Ps. 132:7). Only time would tell the reality of this.

  - o It should also be said, that Ezekiel 43:7 says, that the temple will be the place where the Lord "…dwell[s] in the midst of the children of Israel for ever…". It has been said, that "…for ever…" means, for as long as Israel exists, in physical form, here, on this present earth (2 Chr. 6:2, Eccl. 3:14, Acts 7:48-50). Especially, if there is a literal, end to this present earth's existence (2 Pet. 3:10-11). The point is, our God is always with His faithful followers, wherever He is, we are, and wherever we are, He is, forever!

  - o Zechariah 6:12 talks about the "…BRANCH…" building the temple. It has been said, that this is a term for Jesus. But one must consider what a branch actually is. A branch has many offshoots, and those offshoots are what bear the fruit (John 15:5). So one could suggest, that it may be, the body of Christ, meaning the human remnant of believers, namely, of the descendants of the tribes of Israel, Jew and Gentile believers alike; whom build the "Messianic Age" temple, under the guidance of God's Holy Spirit, the Priests, Levites and the Prince; the "…commonwealth…" of Israel (Prov. 11:28, Dan. 7:27, Eph. 2:12)! Not to mention, there are countless believers here on earth, in the early 21st century A.D., that have already spoken of, planned for, and written about the building of the "Messianic Age" temple; in some form and likeness to each other, that Ezekiel was given a vision of at first (Ezek. 40-48).

o   Zechariah 6:13, may be talking about God dwelling on the "…ark of the covenant…"; that is said, to still exist somewhere on earth today (Deut. 10:8). Where God's throne was in between the two cherubim in the Old Testament and where He spoke from (Lev. 16:2, Num. 7:89, 2 Sam. 6:2, Ps. 80:1). Thus "re-establishing" the authority between the earthly representative of God, through the princely line of the House of David and the heavenly throne of God represented by the Ark of the Covenant here on earth! That all being said, we should never negate the fact, that Jesus Christ of Nazareth, the unmistakable Messiah, only begotten Son of God, has once for all entered into the "…most holy place." with His own sacrificial blood, so that we can dwell with Him wherever we are here on earth and in heaven (Ex. 26:34, Heb. 9:12, 24; 10:19-22)!

o   The last verses I will reference, in respect to the LORD, are Jeremiah 3:16 and 17; it says in Jeremiah 3:16, "…they shall say no more, The ark of the covenant of the LORD: neither shall it come to mind…". This may be for two reason, one is, the possibility that the "…ark of the covenant…" is returned to the "…the most holy place." in the "Messianic Age" built temple, and can only be accessed by the high priests anyhow; but also, because of the fact that Jesus died on the cross for the forgiveness of our sins, shedding His Holy and righteous blood on the cross at Passover in 31 A.D., once for all (Jer. 3:16, Ezek. 41:4, Heb. 10:10). He was buried and He arose the third day, to show us the true way to everlasting life. So indeed, now and forever more the "…ark of the covenant…" is a sign, but the true God and Jesus Christ of Nazareth, are the redeemer and only He can cleanse us of our sins (Jer. 3:16, Heb. 9:12, 24; 10:19-22). And we can dwell with Him, and Him with us, through the indwelling of His Holy Spirit! Jeremiah 3:17 speaks of Jerusalem also, being considered the "…throne of the LORD; and all nations shall be gathered unto it, to the name of the LORD, to Jerusalem…". This description is also likely representative of "…the new Jerusalem…out of heaven…" and God and Jesus Christ of Nazareth, being the temple in it, with God's Holy Spirit (Rev. 21:2, 22). The "Messianic Age" city according to Ezekiel, is just south of the Temple, and can be read about, in more detail, in chapter three and seen depicted in appendix E.

APPENDIX C

1000 years

A 1000 year period of relative peace may be difficult to comprehend for the human mind, especially in this day and age, as of the early 21st century A.D., to imagine the entire world being "good" and obedient to God. However, as was mentioned before, because of the untold damage that would have been done, to this present world's infrastructure; the cleaning up and rebuilding alone, would take some time to finish. Alongside the day to day activities of living, they would keep the inhabitants of earth busy, easily. Above this the worship of God, will in no doubt, be at the forefront of each and every person's daily life, during the "Messianic Age". This may include quite time at home, giving thanks quietly during the work day, or literally visiting Jerusalem during the appointed feast days, namely the Feast of Tabernacles (Zech. 14:16-21). I know in my own life, there have been days that have gone by without notice, and this may very likely be the case, during the "Messianic Age". If, indeed, it is literal, it is a fraction of earth's present history as a whole; but the time spent, will likely be much more peaceful and prosperous, than any other time, in this earth's present history. Something we can all look forward, to thinking about.

That all being said, Revelation 20:7 says, that after the 1000 years is finished, Satan will be loosed out of prison. Here in lays the challenge, there will be one last "battle" at the end of this 1000 years, if it is indeed literal, when "...Gog and Magog...gather...to battle...and compassed the camp of the saints about, and the beloved city: and fire came down from God out of heaven, and devoured them." (Rev. 20:8, 9). This would indeed, in all likelihood, be very similar to what Ezekiel prophesied of in Ezekiel 38 and 39. However, if the Scriptures are taken literally, this would be at the very "...end..." of earth's present history, when God brings the final judgement on all of mankind, resurrecting all whom ever lived, and "...books were opened..." (Matt. 10:22, Rev. 20:10-15). That time, will likely come so quickly, no one may even recognize it. It could even be like a giant asteroid hitting the earth, and all of mankind being physically removed from earth (2 Pet. 3:10-12, Rev. 20:9, 11). This all remains to be seen, of course. There are some New and Old Testament verses that would describe that time; namely, 2 Peter 3:10-12, Revelation 20:9 and 11, Jeremiah 4:23, etc.. But it is not the purpose of this book to go into detail, about the very end of earth's present history. Putting our trust in, submitting to and following Jesus Christ of Nazareth, the only begotten Son of God, through His Holy Spirit, are most important for us to endure life today, and to the "end" of our physical life here on earth, regardless of what plan God has for us, or the inhabits of earth, in this age, or in any other, after it.

Nevertheless, the most important thing to remember, in all of this, is that Jesus Christ came, to save us (John 3:16). He openly suggested that His kingdom is not of this world, and that where He goes, He is preparing a place for us (John 14:3, 18:36). At the very end of the Bible, there is spoken of a "...new heaven and a new earth..." and a "...new Jerusalem...", where all of God's faithful will dwell (Rev. 21:1, 2). Where there is "...no more death, neither sorrow, nor crying, neither shall there be any more pain..." (Rev. 21:4, 5). This is, the Jerusalem, we should ultimately be seeking. The place that "…Eye hath not seen, nor ear heard, neither have entered into the heart of man, the things which God hath prepared for them that love him. But God hath revealed *them* unto us by his Spirit: for the Spirit searcheth all things, yea, the deep things of God." (1 Cor. 2:9, 10). Remember, that this earthly life, is just that, earthly; Jesus Christ of Nazareth is preparing a place for you and I in His heavenly Kingdom for eternity! A place of great wonder and enjoyment! With that all being said, "…let us run with patience the race that is set before us…" (Heb. 12:1).

APPENDIX D

Land Distribution

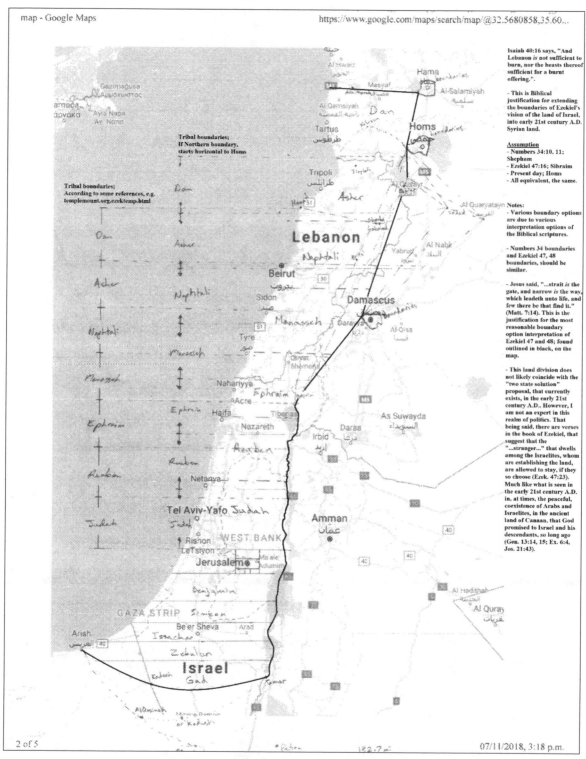

Tribal boundaries;
If Northern boundary,
starts horizontal to Homs

Tribal boundaries;
According to some references, e.g.
templemount.org.ezektemp.html

Isaiah 40:16 says, "And Lebanon *is* not sufficient to burn, nor the beasts thereof sufficient for a burnt offering.".

- This is Biblical justification for extending the boundaries of Ezekiel's vision of the land of Israel, into early 21st century A.D. Syrian land.

Assumption
- Numbers 34:10, 11; Shepham
- Ezekiel 47:16; Sibraim
- Present day; Homs
- All equivalent, the same.

Notes:
- Various boundary options are due to various interpretation options of the Biblical scriptures.

- Numbers 34 boundaries and Ezekiel 47, 48 boundaries, should be similar.

- Jesus said, "...strait *is* the gate, and narrow *is* the way, which leadeth unto life, and few there be that find it." (Matt. 7:14). This is the justification for the most reasonable boundary option interpretation of Ezekiel 47 and 48; found outlined in black, on the map.

- This land division does not likely coincide with the "two state solution" proposal, that currently exists, in the early 21st century A.D.. However, I am not an expert in this realm of politics. That being said, there are verses in the book of Ezekiel, that suggest that the "...stranger..." that dwells among the Israelites, whom are establishing the land, are allowed to stay, if they so choose (Ezek. 47:23). Much like what is seen in the early 21st century A.D. in, at times, the peaceful, coexistence of Arabs and Israelites, in the ancient land of Canaan, that God promised to Israel and his descendants, so long ago (Gen. 13:14, 15; Ex. 6:4, Jos. 21:43).

Google Map, Land allotments

Original map from: https://www.google.com/maps/search/
map/@32.5680858,35.60..., retrieved November 11, 2018.

APPENDIX E

Holy Portion

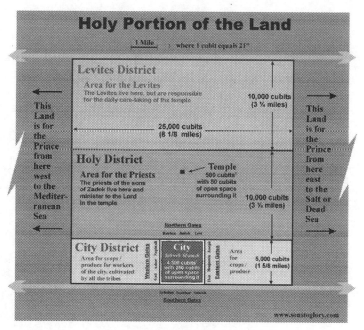

Priestly Land allotment

http://www.sonstoglory.com/ThirdTempleEzekielsMillennialTemple.
htm, retrieved May 02, 2016. Used by permission.

APPENDIX F

Levitical Priesthood

The Levitical priesthood is just that, people from the tribe of Levi. There were 12 tribes of Israel, sons of Jacob, that were blessed, and "called" for various duties within the Israelite community (Gen. 48, 49; Deut. 33). The Levites were chosen to be the priestly class, whom would work in the temple, on behalf of God and the people, Moses and Aaron being the for runners (Ex. 3:10, 28:1, Deut. 33:8-11). Although Levi, early in his life, had taken some matters into his own hands, with his brother Simeon, and Jacob, prophesied over them for that (Gen. 34, 49:5-7). They have become God's chosen vessels, to minister to Him in His physical temple, here on earth (Num. 3, 4). Again, we can all be "...kings and priests..." through Jesus Christ of Nazareth, but that should not "destroy" the special place God has, for the tribe of Levi, in His heart, here on earth (1 Pet. 2:9, Rev. 1:6, 5:10). Every person has been given a particular gift or gifts, tribe or no tribe; by God (Ex. 28:3, 1 Pet. 4:10). As the Bible says, "...we are many members in one body..." (Rom. 12:4, 5; 1 Cor. 12:12). We do not all necessarily have every gift, but as we learn and "perfect" our gifts, the body of Christ functions "better"; and we grow in the unity of God, the Father, through Christ Jesus of Nazareth, God's only begotten Son, with His Holy Spirit (Eph. 4:11-13)!

Zadok

In Ezekiel's prophecy, a specific group of Levites are mentioned; that is the sons of Zadok (Ezek. 40:46, 43:19, 44:15, and 48:11). Zadok was an actual person, in the Old Testament, so presumably his descendants remain on this earth today; just the same as descendants from the other tribes, and descendants of sons from within each tribe, would remain today (1 Chr. 24:3, 27:17, 29:22). Now in regards to this becoming a reality in the future. How might these descendants know that they have been chosen to perform these duties in the "Messianic Age"? As of the early 21st century A.D., there actually exists a school for this similar training, how aware of the Ezekiel prophecies this school is, I do not know (Eph. 3:20). But regardless, these people will undoubtedly be called by God, to these priestly positions and duties. Just like people are "called" to a specific job, or vocation, in the "secular" world; and the modern day religious ministries alike. These will undoubtedly "sense" a strong calling to fulfill a priestly duty in a yet to be built "Messianic Age" temple, as of the early 21st century A.D. (Rom. 8:29, 30).

Just like we need to take steps forward in our faith relationship with God, in whatever we do today. These people will, in all likelihood, do the same (Heb. 11). On a purely physical level, there has been some DNA testing done, on ancestry, and people have been able to trace their roots back, to certain groups of people. Not to mention, the fact that some people's genealogies, including surnames; have indications of tribal affiliation, to various groups, of common ancestry. Regardless, I would suggest, that if these positions are literally going to be fulfilled in the future, that those whom will fill those positions, will have an obvious spiritual calling by

God, through the Holy Spirit, to do so. I would also suggest, that these same people, may also have recognized Jesus Christ of Nazareth, as their Messiah; in order to do their priestly duties, in the proper "spirit". That is, recognizing that the offerings they offer, if literal, are not to take away peoples sins, as individuals; but just that, an offering to God, and more importantly, they are to be eaten and enjoyed as we do at home and in public food establishments, today.

Singers

The singers are special, in that they are mentioned in the Old Testament to be sons of Levi; and seem to be from Asaph, but also from Heman, and Ethan, all descendants of Levi (1 Chr. 15:17-24, Neh. 11:22). These are among the same descendants; whose father, Asaph, was the head of David's worship team (1 Chr. 16:7). This is amazing to think about, because the temple, mentioned in Ezekiel's prophecies, would likely be "run" 100% by the descendants of Levi, the tribe of Levi. This has been the case in the past, and was promised to be the case, as Moses blessed them (Deut. 33:8-11).

Another comment should be said, regarding these singers. David spoke in Psalm 69 of the importance of singing to and praising God, and that it pleases God, "…better than an ox *or* bullock…" (Ps. 69:30, 31). The point here is, that, this is, indeed, the truth; praising and worshipping God in spirit and in truth, is much greater than any physical offering, we can give to God, here on earth. God is a Spirit, and we are to worship Him in spirit and in truth, first and foremost (John 4:24). Alleluia and praise the LORD. Amen and Amen.

APPENDIX G

Ezekiel Temple

Temple

1. Outer Court – Ezekiel 40:17-19
2. Inner Court – Ezekiel 40:44, 47
3. The Temple or Sanctuary – Ezekiel 41:1-26
4. Wall around the outside of the Temple – Ezekiel 40:5, 42:15-20, 45:2
5. Fifty cubits of open space – Ezekiel 45:2

http://www.sonstoglory.com/ThirdTempleEzekielsMillennialTemple.htm, retrieved May 2, 2016. Used by permission.

Note: These are an artist's depiction or interpretation of the Ezekiel 40-46 description of the Ezekiel Temple. The author does not claim these images to be 100% accurate, although there are numerous models built by separate people, which do seem to confirm their accuracy. Also, the river streaming from the temple is not depicted in this model, but would flow in the direction of numbers 2, 1, and 4, and out east, likely along the Kidron valley, to the Dead Sea (Ezek. 47:1-12).

Another website reference on the subject is: http://www.templemount.org/ezektmp.html

READER'S GUIDE:
HOW TO USE THIS BOOK

This book was written with order in mind, so reading it once through first, may be a good idea. There may be some subjects, in the end, that are of more interest, or need more clarification; where you may desire to review them for a better understanding. Part of the reason why the "appendices" exist, is to expand on some of the topics written about in this book, so referring to them may be desired. When writing the book, I had in mind, I was reaching out to a younger generation, but the truth of the matter is, we are all children of God, no matter what age we are. Some of the topics discussed, are not usually talked about, at least commonly weekly, in Church or in the home, at least that I know of; so they may be new to the reader. And it may take some time, to discern, how to apply them to daily life.

The question section attempts to do this, at least in part, by opening back up the readers mind to the Holy Spirit of God. So that you can pray about, meditate on and discuss with others, the subjects spoken about. Although the topics in this book have been spoken about and continue to be spoken about, by various students of; the Bible, God, and Jesus Christ of Nazareth with His Holy Spirit, around the world; the reality of this subject will only be fully known in God's timing. In order to better understand our place with God, life, family and this world; we need to grow in our understanding of somethings. Hopefully, most of the subjects will be simple enough to understand, that not much contemplation is needed; because God does desire us to become like little children, in our relationship with Him and others (Mark 10:15). So with that being said, pray about, meditate on and discuss the ideas that interest you, with whom God wills; and see if you can come to some peace in these matters. God bless and keep the faith!

Chapter 1: The Purpose – Reader's Guide

Discussion: Rest

"So when the Man comes there will be no, no doom."
– Bob Marley, One Love

It is interesting the world we live as of the early 21st century A.D.; so many people, from so many different cultures, religions, languages and nations. How can we possibly all get along? When I was younger, I used to listen to Bob Marley quite a bit, namely during my secondary school days. Although I do not necessarily agree with all of his methods and "philosophies", he was certainly something of a prophet. I am sure he must have read the Bible, and, of course, that comes out in his lyrics to some of his music. Although we must be careful whom we listen to outside of the Bible, and the Holy Spirit; the Bible does admonish to "…believeth all things…" (1 Cor. 13:7). That being said, even as Christ followers, we should not toss aside the "secular" world completely; we are to come out of the world, but God can still work through it, and needs us to live in it; this is where discernment of spirits comes in (John 17:18, 1 Cor. 12:10)!

Discussion Questions

1. Some time ago an idea came into my head; that worship was going to be the method in which evil would be cast from earth. Now there are many forms of worship, and you may desire to learn what forms best suit you; but something is to be said about enjoying pleasant music. David calming king Saul's spirit with a harp, is a perfect example (1 Sam. 16:23). With that being said; how can you contribute in a simple way to the praise and worship of your Creator?

   Read Ephesians 5:19 and Colossians 3:16.

   Ephesians 5:19 says, "Speaking to yourselves…"; while Colossians 3:16 says, "…teaching and admonishing one another…". Here is the key; we need to, first, let God work in us, as individuals, and then we can work with each other. This is where worship, meditation, prayer, reading God's Word, the Holy Bible, discipleship, submission to godly authority and mentoring, come in. You can, first, develop your personal relationship with your Creator, and then when you feel ready, start sharing it with others (Phil. 2:12)!

   The Bible says, that God inhabits our praise (Ps. 22:3)! Is this not proof of how God is manifest in our body, mind and soul, through praising Him!? Praise the LORD! Creator of the heavens and the earth!

Encourage self-reflection and fellowship discussion.

2. In this physical world, some of the best ways we consider to be healthier is by eating properly, exercising and working safely. These are all very important acts, we can partake in, to take care of our body; but ultimately we need to nourish our spirit and soul, first and foremost (Matt. 6:25, Matt. 10:28, Rom. 14:17). What type of habits can be started, renewed or grown, that nourish your soul, mind and body? (Hint: Thanksgiving and Prayer are a great start).

    • Prayer – Communication with your Maker.
    • Praise – Acknowledgement of God, as ruler over all.
    • Reading God's Word – God's common way of communicating with us.
    • Fellowshipping with other believers – Listening to and speaking with others about not only God's Word, but the day to day trials and tribulations, that we may experience here on earth.

    Encourage self-reflection and fellowship discussion.

3. What are some forms of love, that we can portray to this world, to show God's love? Review 1 Corinthians 13 to get started.

    Here are a few more verses for you to continue on your search:

    • Luke 6:31, 35
    • John 15:13
    • Romans 12:9
    • Ephesians 5:25
    • 1 Peter 4:8
    • 1 John 4:8

    Encourage self-reflection and fellowship discussion.

Chapter 2: The Remnant – Reader's Guide

Discussion: No other name!

"Be the change you want to see in the world."
– Mahatma Ghandi

I have mentioned Mahatma Ghandi in my other writing, and he is indeed a very interesting character. He was a part of a movement that, generally, used non-violence, as a method of influence to remove a colonizing "power" from his country of birth. Not everything was always "perfect"; he fasted at times, because of violence, and he did eventually die from some opposition. But, he was an example of a servant for a cause, as Jesus Christ of Nazareth was, and is, a servant of God and for man, whom very much suggested to His own disciples, to change; a better word being "repent"; that involves mercy, forgiveness, mourning and turning from our sins to God, the Father, and Jesus Christ of Nazareth, the only begotten Son of God, with His Holy Spirit (Matt. 3:8, 4:17, 20:28, John 15:5)! I think Mahatma Ghandi was basically saying do not be a hypocrite. We can talk all we desire about change, and what should happen, but if we do not change ourselves, then we are just as Jesus would say, "…hypocrites…" (Matt. 23:13). Following God, listening to and obeying His Holy Spirit, is a lifelong conversion process; Ghandi was not perfect and had to learn from his errors, but Jesus was, and is, that perfect servant, leader. That is why we need and have Jesus Christ of Nazareth. He was, and is, that perfect example of a Man to follow; but He was more than a man, He was, and is, the only begotten Son of God. We have Him to follow unto our final day here on earth, and then God willing, unto eternal life in Jesus Christ of Nazareth, at our resurrections, like He has had His (Rom. 8:28-31, Col. 1:15, 16)! This is the one promise and gift not given by any other person here on earth; only in Jesus Christ of Nazareth, do we have eternal life, in His life giving sacrifice on the cross (John 11:25)! We need Jesus Christ of Nazareth to change our mind, body and soul, to receive the glory He received; so that we can also become like Him, children of God, as God created us to be from the beginning (Luke 3:28, 20:36, Rom. 6:23)! As the Bible says, "Neither is there salvation in any other: for there is none other name under heaven given among men, whereby we must be saved." (Acts 4:12). Jesus Christ of Nazareth is that Name above all names, at which every knee should bow and every tongue should confess that Jesus is Lord (Phil. 2:9-11)!

Discussion Questions

1. When referring to the "…remnant of Israel…", who might the Bible be talking about regarding these people (Ezek. 11:13)? Read Zephaniah 3 to start.

   It can be shown, throughout history, that the modern day descendants of Israel, are still on earth today. Not only that, but they are a very prosperous people, thanks to God!

There are many people throughout the 20th and early 21st century A.D. whom have researched the topic, and some have proven, from various references, where the modern descendants of the ancient people of Israel are today; "Symbols of Our Celto-Saxon Heritage", by W.H. Bennet, 1976; is one example. It should be noted, that in 1 Kings 11:26 – 40, the northern 10 tribes of Israel were given over to Jeroboam, a member of one of the northern 10 tribes (1 Kings 11:28). This, after King Solomon's idolatry, removed his heraldry from qualifying to reign over all of Israel (1 Kings 11:11-13). Later, these 10 tribes were taken into captivity themselves, by Assyria, for their own idolatress ways (2 Kings 17). This was about 700 to 800 years before Christ came to earth, conceived by the Holy Spirit, in and born of, the virgin, Mary, espoused to Joseph (Matt. 1:18-25). Raised, a child of Israel, with brothers and sisters (Matt. 13:55, 56; Luke 2:41-52). At the age of about thirty, Jesus began His earthly ministry, healing, forgiving and doing other miracles. And at Passover, He died on the cross for the forgiveness of our sins, shedding His Holy and righteous blood. He was buried, and the third day He arose from the grave, to give us the hope and promise of eternal life in His Holy name.

From these 10 tribes captivity, they must have gone somewhere!? Searching throughout the chronicled religious and secular history books, of the last 3000 years, as of the early 21st century A.D., referencing the Scriptures on the subject, and using some inspiration, there are clear signs as to where they may generally be located on earth today!

Encourage self-reflection and fellowship discussion.

2. If we as God's people are "called" to keep His appointed feast days, mentioned in Leviticus 23. How can we do so, if we are part of a congregation or ecclesiastical organization that does not necessarily outwardly or openly keep these commands on the church calendar?

Depending on where you desire to see yourself in your relationship with God and others, the apostles and Jesus made it clear, that we ought not to be held guilty for any feast we keep or do not keep (Rom. 14:5). But Salvation comes from faith and confession, that Jesus Christ is Lord, the Son of God, and the belief that God raised Him from the dead (Rom. 10:9, Eph. 2:8, 1 John 4:15)!

Nevertheless, if a person, family or community is interested in following the Old Testament festival laws, they are indeed a shadow of things that came and will come (Col. 2:17). So, from my perspective, the easiest way to look at this, is when the Israelites were in the wilderness (Jos. 5:6). They were just starting to develop a "civil" and "religious" structure of their own, apart from the structures of Egypt and the "world", in general; and although there was some "outside" influence for governing infrastructure development, namely Moses' father in law, Jethro. The people, the tribes of Israel, were learning how to live as a "society", under God's rule (Ex. 1:11, 18).

In particular, they were commanded to collect manna 6 days, and an extra amount on the 6th day, for eating on the 7th day, because the 7th day they were to rest, in their places (Ex.

16:29, Num. 1:52). Here is the key, if a person, family or community are thinking about following the feast days of the Old Testament, it must start in the house! First in our heart; body, mind, and soul; and then in our homes with family; and then God willing, in the community at large; and finally, if the prophecies of the Bible are to be fulfilled in a literal sense, with all whom live on earth.

Again though, it must be made clear that salvation does not come from following a law or rule; unless you consider putting your faith in Jesus Christ of Nazareth as your Lord, the only begotten Son of God, and believing He has risen from the dead by God, as a rule or law. In fact it is not a rule or law. We are given the freedom to choose, whether or not we desire to believe in the truth of Jesus Christ of Nazareth and the gift He has for YOU and I (Eph. 2:8). Do you? If so let someone know, even God through prayer; that is the start of your own testimony and walk with Jesus Christ of Nazareth, in you and with you forever more! May the LORD bless you (Num. 6:24-26)!

Encourage self-reflection and fellowship discussion.

3. God says, in the Bible, in various places what will take place in the "…time of the end." (Dan. 12:9). Namely, that He will speak to us in dreams and visions. Although this has been confirmed to have been taking place since the beginning of Christ's resurrection, and even in the Old Testament, through the prophets and kings, etc.; it no doubt continues to take place today. How is God speaking to you? Do you have dreams or "visons" or ideas when resting that may be providing understanding for your future and the future of your loved ones? How should you act on them? Read Acts 2:17 and Joel 2:28 for more insight!

Speaking with someone is always a help. The Bible talks about dreams in different places. Sometimes dreams come from the multitude of ideas we have in our head, from our business (Eccl. 5:3). But sometimes dreams are "prophetic" in nature, and may be "coded" with things, that will happen in the future, and they may contain ideas for how to solve a problem we are having.

It is important not to get hung up on them, or trust in dreams, most importantly (Deut. 13:1-5). God is our Creator, and He is whom we should put our trust in. We have to remember, that our own fleshly mind, and the "adversary", are the enemy of God; and that only God and Jesus Christ of Nazareth, God, the Father's, only begotten Son, through His Holy Spirit, can reveal the truth of dreams or visions, for how to go about our daily life, here on earth (Gen. 40:8, Rom. 8:7).

Encourage self-reflection and fellowship discussion.

Chapter 3: The 3 R's — Reader's Guide

Discussion: The Order of the "Messianic Age"

"To love rightly is to love what is orderly and beautiful
in an educated and disciplined way."
– Plato

A lot has been said in this chapter and there is a lot to digest. As the old saying goes, "Rome was not built in a day". Well the fact of the matter is, this world has not come to this point overnight. We have been building, growing, waring, dying and rebuilding for close to 6000 years, as of the early 21st century A.D.. As we approach the possibility of the dawn of a "Messianic Age", we need to take our time, especially if there are some events that are to come upon this world before it, that will likely shake the earth, like this world has never experienced before, and never will experience again (Matt. 24:21). God is a God of order and decency, we need to follow His lead and do the same (1 Cor. 14:33, 40). This may require repentance on our part, tossing out old ideas that are either complete lies, or are no longer "valid". We need to be thinking about what changes we need to make in our daily, weekly and yearly "routine" and we also need to reconsider our relationship with our Maker and others (Hag. 1:7)! This will not happen overnight, but it took six evenings and mornings to create the earth and all that is in it with God resting on the seventh day, so we also likely have some time (Gen. 1:31-2:3)!

Discussion Questions

1. What types of changes to this world's health system and the way it views patient care might need to take place in order to provide effectively for a world that no longer has major "illnesses", physical or mental, plaguing it any longer? What about other infrastructure systems?

    Read 2 Chronicles 16:12, Psalm 118:8 and Jeremiah 17:5, to start.

    Encourage self-reflection and fellowship discussion.

2. Does God really like order? How about a proper education system? What can we do about it?

    Read 1 Corinthians 14:33, 40 and Genesis 1.

Encourage self-reflection and fellowship discussion.

3. Imagining a time when all people are at some sort of agreement on religious issues. It may sound like a "pipe dream" in the world we live in, as of the early 21st century A.D., but it seems God will bring something like this about. What can we do in the meantime while we are waiting or "working" towards this goal of peace on earth?

    Review Psalm 27:14, Zechariah 14:16-19, Matthew 26:41, Galatians 5:15 and Philippians 2:12, to start.

    Encourage self-reflection and fellowship discussion.

Chapter 4: The Government – Reader's Guide

Discussion: Of God and Man

"As I would not be a slave, so I would not be a master. This expresses my idea of democracy."
– Abraham Lincoln, 16th US President

Abraham Lincoln, an early President of the United States of America, and a helper in the abolishing of slavery. His words ring very true today, and are exactly how Jesus feels about us. He said, "Henceforth I call you not servants; for the servant knoweth not what his lord doeth: but I have called you friends…" (John 15:15). Jesus' only desire is that we turn to Him, is that we commune with Him, is that we believe in Him and that ultimately, we accept the incredible gift of eternal life in His Holy name (1 Tim. 2:3, 4). His work was already complete on the cross (John 17:4, 19:30). He does not have to do anything else, His earthly suffering for us, was momentary; but His life is eternal, and so can ours be, through accepting the sacrifice He made for us so many years ago (John 16:20-22, 2 Cor. 4:17). He loves us, and desires us to be like Him! To live forever, to be children of the living God! Whom does not change and who has everything, "…with whom is no variableness, neither shadow of turning." (Mal. 3:6, Eph. 4:6, Jam. 1:17). If we had only God's Holy Spirit in us, and had nothing else, we would and do have everything! God's Holy Spirit is the seed of eternal life, it is the seed of all that we see and cannot see (Gal. 3:29, 1 Pet. 1:23, 1 John 3:9). It is so simple, yet so difficult for some to understand, and yet really, we are not called to fully understand God right from the start, we are just called to accept Him and trust Him; one step at a time, so to speak (Jos. 1:8, Job 23:12, Ps. 119:15, Luke 24:45, 1 Cor. 2:9-12, 1 Pet. 2:2). This is the peace of God that passes all understanding (Phil. 4:7)! Understanding, knowledge and having an answer for every question under the sun is great, but it is the peace of God, His rest, that is infinite, eternal and wonderful; a goal worth working towards (Phil. 3:14)! In Jesus Christ of Nazareth, we have that peace; in God's Holy Spirit we have that peace; in God, the Father, we have peace (Isa. 9:6, Rom. 5:1, 2 Thess. 3:16)!

Discussion Questions

1. How can only 144 000 be chosen? What about all of the other Christ followers throughout history? (Hint: Ephesians 2:19).

   Ephesians 2:19 says, "Now therefore ye are no more strangers and foreigners, but **fellowcitizens** with the saints, and of the household of God…".

Also Revelation 7:9-17 talks about the "...great multitude..." coming out of "...great tribulation...". You may desire to look into these verses.

The point is, we are all a part of God's family, if we follow Him, and we will all receive the gifts He promises us, whether you or I think we deserve to be classified as "saints", in this life, or another life, or not.

Encourage self-reflection and fellowship discussion.

2. Does the epistle to the Hebrews give a clue to whom will physically be "ruling" earth during the "Messianic Age"? Read Hebrews 2:5-12 to start.

    Encourage self-reflection and fellowship discussion.

3. If God can make an animal speak, can He not also guide man in ruling this world? Read Numbers 22:28-30 and find other verses that confirm God's sovereignty over all of His creation.

    Some more verses on the topic: 2 Peter 2:14 and Jeremiah 10:23.

    God has control over us whether we like to believe it or not. Yes we have free will and we can chose to do wrong, but ultimately, the Holy Spirit of God prevails!

    Encourage self-reflection and fellowship discussion.

Chapter 5: The Temple – Reader's Guide

Discussion: Jesus' Sacrifice

"Happiness and moral duty are inseparably connected."
– George Washington

This chapter was filled with ideas about law, service, offerings, atonement for sin, etc.. Although some may be more interested in the information of this chapter than others, and may desire to learn more about these concepts outside of the writing of this book; it is important to remember that Jesus Christ of Nazareth died on the cross for the forgiveness of the sins, shedding His Holy and righteous blood for us. He was buried and He arose the third day, to give us all the opportunity to receive eternal life in His Holy name, like He has received from God, the Father (John 11:25, 26; Rom. 5:8, 8:11)! This was God's ultimate goal from the beginning, to create mankind in His image, after His likeness (Gen. 1:27, Eph. 4:24, Col. 3:10). God is eternal and He desires us to be as well (John 17:3, 1 Tim. 1:17, 1 John 2:17). This requires that we follow Jesus Christ of Nazareth, accept His atonement for the forgiveness of our sins, and obey Him to the end of our natural life, here on earth, and forever more in the world to come (John 13:34, 15:12; Heb. 10). Because ultimately, this life is not the end of the journey, it is just the beginning. What Jesus desires, is a repentant heart (Ps. 51:17, Matt. 4:17, 9:13). If you are reading this chapter and are questioning whether you are worthy of such a sacrifice the answer is no, but do not worry, Jesus died for us while we were yet sinners (Rom. 5:8, 2 Tim. 1:9, 10, 1 John 4:10). God loves you as a sinner, He desires us to change and become like Him, but He loves you as you are today (John 3:16). The Bible says, "That if thou shalt confess with thy mouth the Lord Jesus, and shalt believe in thine heart that God hath raised him from the dead, thou shalt be saved." (Rom. 10:9). Even this is a gift from God, the faith required to believe is given by God, all you need to do is accept it (Eph. 2:8)! How simple is salvation in Jesus Christ of Nazareth.

Discussion Questions

1. What about the law, was it not "done away with" when Christ came? Look up some New Testament scriptures that verify your argument.

   Jesus said of Himself, "Think not that I am come to destroy the law, or the prophets: I am not come to destroy, but to fulfil. For verily I say unto you, Till heaven and earth pass, one jot or one tittle shall in no wise pass from the law, till all be fulfilled." (Matt. 5:17, 18). See also Romans 7.

Nevertheless, Hosea 6:6 makes clear, what God desires of us, first and foremost; mercy and the knowledge of God. Jesus Christ of Nazareth is filled with grace and truth (John 1:17). He is asking the same of us, as well!

Encourage self-reflection and fellowship discussion.

2. What about the princely line? Is David going to be resurrected to become leader of the 12 tribes of Israel in the "Messianic Age"? Or is a descendant of His family or possibly from another tribe going to be this prince? What do you think? Find some Scriptures to help you with your understanding.

Some "Messianic Age" commentators have suggested that David will be resurrected and sit on his throne again as king of the tribes of Israel (Ezek. 34:23, 24). This may be possible, but we must remember two things. First, Jesus fulfilled and inherited David's throne for eternity, because He was from the family line of David; but is also the eternal, only begotten Son of God (Mark 11:10, Luke 1:32, Heb. 7:24). And second, the Old Testament speaks in more than one place, of David's seed inheriting the throne "…for evermore.", if they follow God (Ps. 132:11, 12). So regardless of whether David is revealed physically with the rest of the saints or not, his throne will remain through his descendants physically and through Jesus Spiritually!

Read Psalm 132 for more on this promise.

Encourage self-reflection and fellowship discussion.

3. This chapter touched on sacrifices and offerings. Although these may be literal or they may not be, in the "Messianic Age". What is God really looking for, in us, and from us, besides offering Him physical sacrifices and offerings? (Hint: Review Psalm 51:17 and Matthew 9:13 for insight).

There are many more verses like them, such as; 1 Samuel 15:22, Jeremiah 7:22, 23; Hosea 6:6, Micah 6:6-8, etc.. Read them through, and ask God to give you understanding, in what He is actually asking of you, and your life's purpose, here on earth, and forever after!

Isaiah 66 is a sobering chapter in Isaiah's book. Read it, to find out what God is looking for, in your personal relationship with Him.

Encourage self-reflection and fellowship discussion.

Chapter 6: The Blessings – Reader's Guide

Discussion: Peace

"Of all our dreams today there is none more important - or so hard to realise - than that of peace in the world. May we never lose our faith in it or our resolve to do everything that can be done to convert it one day into reality."
– Lester B. Pearson

Peace may seem like a far off dream to some. But I know, from experience that a person can experience it; if even only as an individual with our Maker, in Jesus Christ of Nazareth, and coming to a place of contentment with our life circumstances, in general (1 Tim. 6:6, 7). As really, this is the only way we will ever truly experience peace (Ps. 29:11, 34:14, 37:37, 85:8, 119:165; John 14:27, 16:33). Jesus Christ of Nazareth is the author and finisher of our faith; we cannot write our own "book of life" for Him, we have to let Him write our name in His "… book of life…" (Heb. 12:2, Rev. 20:12). This is the key, and will be the key to peace on earth; it will be the submission of mankind, slowly but surely, to the Almighty God and Creator, through Jesus Christ of Nazareth, God, the Father's, only begotten Son, denying ourselves, taking up our cross daily and following Jesus (Luke 2:14, 9:23). We must be alert and watching, because Jesus Christ said, there would arise false prophets and people would say, here He is or there He is, at the end of the "world" or "ages" (Matt. 24:24-27). I know I have listened to many different teachers of the Bible and Bible prophecy; and certainly they have all had some knowledge, as the Bible says "… we know in part, and we prophesy in part.", but the ultimate teacher is Jesus Christ Immanuel of Nazareth and His Holy Spirit, with God, the Father (1 Cor. 13:9, Rev. 19:10). He has a still small voice and He will speak to you! In Joel and the book of Acts, it says that, the Holy Spirit would be poured out on all flesh in the latter days, people would dream dreams, have visions and prophecy (Joel 2:28, Acts 2:17). Rest assured that the "ALL", includes you! God bless, and keep the faith (1 Tim. 6:12, 2 Tim. 4:7).

Discussion Questions

1. Have you ever heard the term "peace and quiet"? Such as, someone is looking for peace and quiet. This comes from God; this is a fruit of the kingdom of God! Find some verses in the Bible, that would suggest this is the truth. (Hint: to get started look at Proverbs 17:1, 28 and Exodus 14:14).

   Here are some other verses that may help you with your understanding:

   • Psalm 37:7

- Psalm 46:10
- Lamentations 3:26
- Zephaniah 3:9
- Ephesians 4:29

Encourage self-reflection and fellowship discussion.

2. How can we receive all of these blessings, if Jesus is not "literally" walking this earth, with us, in a "Messianic Age"? (Hint: think about who was sent to us after Jesus ascended to heaven).

John 16 is very clear on the subject of what Jesus was up to, whom He is, what His relationship is with God and whom Jesus sent to us to be with us forever; namely, His Holy Spirit, the Comforter. This is why it is important, that we do not ignore or rebel continually; against God's Holy Spirit working in us, the Bible, this world and other people around us, because He is our life and life more abundantly (John 10:10)!

Encourage self-reflection and fellowship discussion.

3. Prayer, Praise, learning and action. These are all keys to "reaping the harvest" of God's abundance in our life! He created us, not to sit and do nothing at all, and just "will" all the blessings into our life; but we need to do some sort of "work" or "deed" in order to receive many of these physical blessings (Jam. 2:20, 26). That being said, miracles do still happen, so do not discount the unexplainable blessings you receive either; especially the gift of eternal life, that none of us can earn of our own efforts (Rom. 6:23, Eph. 2:8, 9)! What type of godly actions can you take, to receive the blessings you desire, for yourself and others?

John 17:9, 20 and 21 say, that Jesus prayed not only for His disciples, but also for all those that believe after them, so that we may all be one. Is this not great news! Jesus thought about you before you were even born into this world, and prayed for you if you believe it, do you?!

Jesus is in us, and we can know God, the Father, through Him, with His Holy Spirit dwelling in us (John 17:25, 26)!

Encourage self-reflection and fellowship discussion.

Chapter 7: The Conclusion – Reader's Guide

Discussion: Life

"…I am come that they may have life, and that they may have *it* more abundantly."
– Jesus Christ of Nazareth, John 10:10

The Bible says, "…at the name of Jesus every knee should bow…And *that* every tongue should confess that Jesus Christ *is* Lord…" (Phil. 2:10, 11). This does not necessarily mean that they will be saved, because Jesus said, not everyone that says, "…Lord, Lord…" will enter into the kingdom of heaven (Matt. 7:21). Even though everyone is God's, and God has created everything, and everyone for His purpose; we must truly and earnestly desire Him, listen to Him and follow Him daily, to receive the abundance of life. The truth is, that this life is only a small amount of time; we can try and "jam" in all kinds of material things, people and experiences, but we must also consider that God is giving us much more than this life here on earth (Rev. 21:7). He is giving us a life, that will not perish (John 11:26). We may "die" someday, but ultimately we will have a resurrected body if we obey God and follow Jesus Christ of Nazareth, with His Holy Spirit, to the end (John 3:16). He will give us the life that does not die; He will give us an incorruptible body, that will last forever (1 Cor. 15:53). Jesus said, "In my Father's house are many mansions: if *it were* not *so,* I would have told you. I go to prepare a place for you. And if I go and prepare a place for you, I will come again, and receive you unto myself; that where I am, *there* ye may be also." (John 14:2, 3). It may not be 100% obvious, where that place is today; but I suspect it will be like the "…garden of Eden…", as the Bible says, "… a new heaven and a new earth…" (Gen. 2:15, Isa. 65:17, Rev. 21:1). The point is, that life in Jesus Christ of Nazareth is abundant, because it will last forever!

Discussion Questions

1. With all of these ideas, "rules" and changes that may be required in order to fulfil the reality of the ideas written about in this book, regarding the "Messianic Age"; how can we live the truth of the lessons of the Bible, based on some of these more detailed "prophecies", without losing sight of the simple message, that the Bible ultimately puts forth?

    One of the most valid verses that can be leaned on, in the New Testament, for this is, "But I fear, lest by any means, as the serpent beguiled Eve through his subtlety, so your minds should be corrupted from the simplicity that is in Christ." (2 Cor. 11:3). The point is, that we need not get caught up in the "law" or the "rituals" or the "works" in order to save us (Rom. 3). Salvation is a gift from God, and it was given to us through His only begotten Son, Jesus Christ of Nazareth (Eph. 1:1-14). This is the most important thing to remember, regardless of what our daily, weekly, monthly and yearly routine is here on earth, literal "Messianic Age" or not.

Encourage self-reflection and fellowship discussion.

1. If Jesus was, is and is to come, the Lamb of God, whom sacrificed Himself once for all, for the forgiveness of our sins; how could God ever accept animal offerings again? See Psalm 22:29 to start.

    Psalm 51, especially the verses 16 to 19, have some interesting insight into this idea. God is looking for, in us, a broken and contrite, meaning repentant, spirit. He desires us to turn from our sins, before we offer Him a physical offering for our repentance (Matt. 5:24)!

    Christ came amongst us, while we were still sinners, but He knew that we needed Him, so He sacrificed Himself for us (1 John 3:16)! Jesus said of Himself, "...I am the bread of life..." (John 6:35). He is also speaking about Himself, in comparison to the manna that came down from heaven, while the Israelites were sojourning in the wilderness forty years, before coming into the land of Canaan, promised to them, in approximately 1500 B.C. (Exodus, Numbers, Joshua). But Jesus is the true manna, He gives us life and life more abundantly (John 6:32-35, 10:10). These words likely fulfill the representation of using unleavened bread at the time of the feast of unleavened bread, during Passover, and during the seven days after; the similar time of year, better known in the west, as "Easter", as of the early 21st century A.D.. Removing the old yeast and eating unleavened bread is another reminder to repent and remove sin from our life (1 Cor. 5:7)! With the help of Jesus' eternal sacrifice and His Holy Spirit working in and through us, we can all do this easily and as often as needed (Matt. 11:29, 30; 26:26-29, 1 Cor. 11:23-26)!

    Encourage self-reflection and fellowship discussion.

1. In the end, we need to focus on the "main thing"; that is, Jesus died on the cross for the forgiveness of our sins at Passover. He was buried, and He arose three days later, to show us that we also can live forever, if we believe in and follow Him, whole heartedly to the end. What changes or new "practices" can you make in your daily routine, to better reflect, a life lived for Jesus Christ of Nazareth, God's only begotten Son, and God, the Father, through His Holy Spirit, first and foremost?

    As has been mentioned in my book, "Seven Steps to Freedom"; we need to keep God's Word with us, every day, and we do this by reading His Word, the Holy Bible, and praying to God, in Christ Jesus of Nazareth's Holy name, God, the Father's, only begotten Son, and through worshiping and praising Him, and giving Him thanksgiving. We can hear from Him, through reading Scripture, and we can also hear the still small voice of His Holy Spirit, to commune with God, the Father, in Christ Jesus of Nazareth's Holy name. We should also fellowship with fellow believers, so that the Holy Spirit is able to complete our purpose here on earth; that is, to participate in and be a part of the Body of Christ, the Church of the living God!

Encourage self-reflection and fellowship discussion.

ABOUT THE AUTHOR

He has a University education in civil engineering, and has self-published two previous books with Westbow press.

Printed in the United States
by Baker & Taylor Publisher Services